FOSTERING GEOMETRIC THINKING

FOSTERING GEOMETRIC THINKING

A Guide for Teachers, Grades 5–10

Mark Driscoll

with Rachel Wing DiMatteo, Johannah Nikula, and Michael Egan
of Education Development Center, Inc.

HEINEMANN
Portsmouth, NH

Heinemann

361 Hanover Street
Portsmouth, NH 03801–3912
www.heinemann.com

Offices and agents throughout the world

This work was supported by the National Science Foundation under Grant NO EHR-0353409. Any opinions, findings, conclusions, or recommendations here are those of the authors and do not necessarily reflect the views of the National Science Foundation.

Library of Congress Cataloging-in-Publication Data
Driscoll, Mark J.
  Fostering geometric thinking : a guide for teachers, grades 5–10 / Mark Driscoll ; with Rachel Wing DiMatteo, Johannah Nikula, and Michael Egan.
     p. cm.
  Includes bibliographical references and index.
  ISBN-13: 978-0-325-01148-6
  ISBN-10: 0-325-01148-6
  1. Geometry—Study and teaching (Secondary). I. DiMatteo, Rachel Wing.
II. Nikula, Johannah. III. Egan, Michael. IV. Title.
  QA461.D75   2007
   372.7—dc22   2007027581

Editor: Victoria Merecki
Production editor: Sonja S. Chapman
Cover design: Bernadette Skok
Compositor: Publishers' Design and Production Services, Inc.
DVD production: Kevin Carlson
Manufacturing: Steve Bernier

Printed in the United States of America on acid-free paper
11   VP   3 4 5

Contents

Acknowledgments

This long list of acknowledgments reflects the immense amount of helpful feedback we have received while putting together this book and its associated materials, the *Fostering Geometric Thinking Toolkit*. First we want to acknowledge the National Science Foundation for its support of our efforts.

Next, we are grateful to our colleagues and fostering geometric thinking (FGT) collaborators at Horizon Research, Inc., especially Dan Heck who captained the FGT research component and gave us numerous insights into teacher learning. We are also grateful to our Education Development Center (EDC) colleagues for their support throughout the project: June Mark, Deborah Spencer, Grace Kelemanik, Amy Busey, Lauren May, and Amy May—the person who worked steadily behind the scenes to keep the communication flowing.

We are grateful to advisory board members—Patrick Callahan, Al Cuoco, Naomi Fisher, Martin Gartzman, Joan Kenney, Richard Lehrer, Nora Ramirez, Regeta Slaughter, and Jane Swafford—for their keen interest in our work and their insightful suggestions for revising materials and for studying their impact.

Our efforts during the first year of the project were helped immensely by a group of savvy Collaborating Teachers: Michelle Allman, JoAnne Billings, Barbara Fox, Betsy Gavron, Kristen Herbert, Kelly Hagen McCormack, Joanne Rose, Michael Smalley, Sandy Stymiest, Barbara Swidler, and Ellen Viruleg.

Field-test facilitators provided invaluable feedback, as well as a variety of records of student work on FGT problems: Ann Altman, John Baer, Barbara Cardano, Kathi Chlanda, Anne Cook, Andrea Doyle, Christopher Fraley, Betsy Gavron, Lori Gibson, Jeanne Glover, Leslie Good, John Hart, Debbie Hill, Karen Hyma, Shawnda Johnson, Sherry Lane, Maureen Mason, Kelly Hagan McCormack, Jean McGehee, Lynne Mendes, Rita Messer, Pam Mulson, Caroline Neel, Marianne O'Connor, Jerry Pomeroy, Judy Pomeroy, Annmarie Sargent, Joy Ramirez, Michael Smalley, Paula Smith, Deborah Underwood, and Ernest Yago.

Both the book and materials have been enriched by a set of videotaped records of students working on FGT problems. For video contributions, we are particularly grateful to the students and teachers in Attleboro, Brookline, Clinton, Newton, and Wayland, MA; Lexington, SC; Bismarck, ND; and especially to those in Lawrence, MA, where the majority of videos were recorded. The brightness, enthusiasm, persistence, and charm of the students in these clips, as they worked on FGT problems, may be the best argument of all for more attention to geometry in the middle grades.

Introduction

In 1982, Sir Michael Atiyah addressed a group of mathematicians on the topic "What is geometry?" Atiyah—renowned Oxford mathematician, Fields Medalist, and winner of the 2004 Abel Prize—offered the view that effective mathematical problem solving depends on complementary ways of thinking:

> Broadly speaking I want to suggest that geometry is that part of mathematics in which visual thought is dominant whereas algebra is that part in which sequential thought is dominant. This dichotomy is perhaps better conveyed by the words *insight* versus *rigour* and both play an essential role in real mathematical problems.
>
> The educational implications of this are clear. We should aim to cultivate and develop both modes of thought. It is a mistake to overemphasise one at the expense of the other and I suspect that geometry has been suffering in recent years. (Atiyah 2003, 29)

The following may illustrate his point about the two complementary modes of thought.

→ The straight line $y = (\frac{7}{12})x + \frac{1}{4}$ passes through two points with integer coordinates $(3, 2)$ and $(-9, -5)$. Are there other points on this straight line with both coordinates integers?

One way to think about the problem has a sequential feel to it and is grounded in attention to the numerical relationship between a number x and the number $(\frac{7}{12})x + \frac{1}{4}$:

- Saying $(\frac{7}{12})x + \frac{1}{4}$ is an integer, with x also an integer, implies that $\frac{7x}{12} + \frac{1}{4}$ is an integer, which in turn implies that

- $7x + 3$ is divisible by 12, so

- $7x$ will leave a remainder of 9 when divided by 12

- So, $(x, (\frac{7}{12})x + \frac{1}{4})$ works if and only if x is of the form $3 + 12m$ for some integer m. And this implies that there are

- an infinite number of points on the line with integer coordinates. For example, the two given points, (3, 2) and (−9, −5), correspond to $m = 0$ and $m = −1$, respectively, and this invites thinking about $m = 1$, which yields the next point on the line with integer coordinates, (15, 9).

Another way of thinking about the problem, which seems more visual in character, grows from attending to the role that similar triangles play in the graphs of linear functions. For example, there are infinitely many right triangles, with vertex (−9, −5) and hypotenuse on the line through (−9, −5) and (3, 2), similar to the right triangle with vertices (−9, −5), (3, 2), and (3, −5). To construct such similar triangles, one could double the lengths of the sides of that right triangle, triple them, quadruple them, and so on from which one can see that there are an infinite number of points with integer coordinates on the line (see Figure I–1).

We want students to learn to think in both kinds of ways, so Atiyah's final sentence about "geometry suffering" expresses a sentiment we share, and one that was a strong motivator for writing this book. We believe that U.S. students have been given too little exposure to geometry and geometrical thinking, particularly in the middle grades. We also believe this negligence has had detrimental effects, as recent data show.

FIGURE I–1

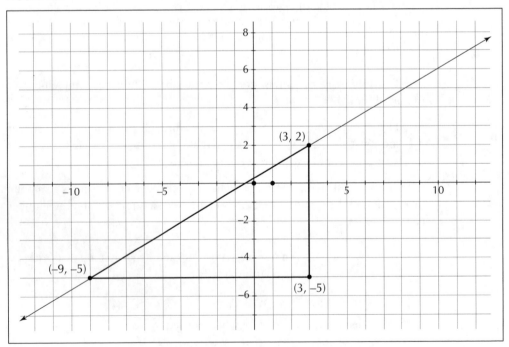

In a summary of research on teaching and learning geometry at the K–12 level, Clements concluded that "U.S. curriculum and teaching in the domain of geometry is generally weak, leading to unacceptably low levels of achievement" (2003, 152). Geometry has been characterized as "the forgotten strand" (Lappan 1999) among those identified in the *Principles and Standards for School Mathematics* (National Council of Teachers of Mathematics 2000).

Beyond shape recognition, geometric concepts have received scant attention in many curriculum materials for grades K–8 (AAAS 2000; NCTM 2000). Teachers may not even teach what little geometry can be found in those materials (Clements 2003; Porter 1989; Fuys, Geddes, and Tischler 1988). Even with curriculum materials that provide opportunity for studying deeper concepts in geometry, teachers may lack knowledge and skills to teach geometry effectively (Goldsmith, Mark, and Kantrov 1998).

The need for improvement in geometry teaching and learning in the middle and high school grades is clearly evident in international comparisons such as Trends in International Mathematics and Science Study (TIMSS), which focuses on grades 4, 8, and 12, and Programme for International Student Assessment (PISA), which compares the performance of 15-year-old students. Consistently over recent years, in TIMSS for grade 8, geometry and measurement are the areas of weakest performances for U.S. students (Ginsburg et al. 2005; Mullis et al. 2001; Beaton et al. 1997). By the end of high school, the scores of U.S. students were near the bottom in the TIMSS study of advanced mathematics, with U.S. geometry performance the lowest of all participating nations (Mullis et al. 1998).

In an analysis of the 2003 TIMSS and PISA assessments, Ginsburg et al. (2005) compared the results in the countries that participated in TIMSS at grades 4 and 8 and in PISA.[1] They concluded that the United States spends 50 percent less time on geometry in grade 8 than the other countries. They concluded also that measurement and geometry were the clear weaknesses: U.S. students' performance on measurement items was statistically lower than their overall score on TIMSS-4 and TIMSS-8; their performance on geometry items was statistically lower than their overall performance on TIMSS-8 and PISA.

There may be a glimmer of hope in all these worrisome data. The same TIMSS–PISA analysis determined that U.S. students' performance on statistics items (e.g., data, probability, uncertainty) was statistically higher than their overall score on TIMSS-4, TIMSS-8, and PISA. Perhaps not by coincidence, it was also determined that the United States spends 50 percent more time on data and statistics at grade 4 than the other countries.

---

[1]The twelve countries that participated in TIMSS-4, TIMSS-8, and PISA are Australia, Belgium, Hong Kong, Hungary, Italy, Japan, Latvia, the Netherlands, New Zealand, Norway, the Russian Federation, and the United States.

All these data provide compelling evidence that:

- We don't teach enough geometry or geometric thinking in the middle grades.

- The effects of this negligence show up in international assessments.

- The opposite is true for statistics: greater relative emphasis in instruction, arguably leads to greater relative results in international comparisons.

The conclusion seems clear: As a country, we need to increase attention to geometry in the middle grades. Further, what students learn should be rich in geometric reasoning.

A recent analysis demonstrated that geometric skills on the TIMSS assessments are definitely related to students' competence with higher-order mathematics processes including: logical reasoning, applications of knowledge in arithmetic and geometry, management of data and procedures, and proportional reasoning. This finding has led to the suggestion that teaching geometric thinking in the middle grades is at least as important as teaching algebraic thinking (Tatsuoka, Corter, and Tatsuoka 2004).

When it comes to deciding how to enrich middle-grades geometry learning, there are sources of guidance to turn to. For example, the Grades 6–8 Geometry and Measurement Standards of the National Council of Teachers of Mathematics (NCTM) use the following phrases to describe learning expectations (NCTM 2000, 232, 240) that portray a very rich diet of geometric learning for students.

- "Analyze characteristics and properties of . . . geometric shapes and develop mathematical arguments about geometric relationships"

- "Describe spatial relationships"

- "Apply transformations"

- "Use visualization, spatial reasoning, and geometric modeling to solve problems"

- "Understand measurable attributes of objects"

Further, in 2006, NCTM complemented the Principles and Standards by describing compact sets of Curriculum Focal Points in each grade through grade 8 (www.nctmmedia.org/cfm). Among the focal points are:

- Grade 5: "Describing three-dimensional shapes and analyzing their properties, including volume and surface area."

- Grade 7: "Understanding and applying proportionality, including similarity."
- Grade 8: "Understanding two- and three-dimensional space and figures using distance and angle."

A central purpose of this book is in its title: to enhance the chances of teachers fostering geometric thinking in their classrooms so that students will learn to use geometric thinking as a complement to algebraic thinking in problem solving. Teachers' understanding of geometric thinking, along with their ability to help students understand and employ geometric thinking, seems like a very important piece of school mathematics.

In its 2005 book, *How Students Learn Mathematics in the Classroom*, the National Research Council offered three core principles for success in mathematics instruction: (1) engaging prior understandings, (2) organizing knowledge around core concepts, and (3) supporting metacognition. It is our view that metacognition, particularly in the area of geometry, is hardly visible in school mathematics. Fostering students' attention to their geometric thinking to help them think more productively when solving problems is very important.

We believe, however, that a prerequisite to teachers accomplishing this goal is their own understanding of geometric thinking. Those two goals for teachers—*understanding geometric thinking* and *fostering geometric thinking*—are at the heart of this book. The following features are intended to help in this regard.

- *Chapter 1, Geometric Habits of Mind*, contains a description of productive geometric thinking in terms of four geometric habits.

An organization around three clusters of topics that echo the NCTM recommendations follows:

- *Chapter 2, Geometric Relationships:* Just as important in problem solving as algebraic thinking about numerical relationships is geometric thinking about relationships within and between geometric figures. (Consider, for example, the relationship between each of the similar triangles considered in solving the problem about finding points on the straight line with both coordinates integers.)

- *Chapter 3, Geometric Transformations*, with emphasis on their effect on geometric objects, particularly invariance effects. For example, does a particular transformation preserve length-of-line segments? Does it preserve area?

- *Chapter 4, Geometric Measurement*, considers measuring such as the length, area, angle, size, and volume.

A summary of recommendations for instructional practice wraps up this book:

- *Chapter 5, Principles for Fostering Geometric Thinking,* makes principles that have been implicit in previous chapters explicit: a steady diet of geometric problem solving is valuable for middle graders; focusing on communication in middle-grades geometry is important; and middle-grades geometry can and should form the groundwork for high school geometry.

Accompanying this book is a DVD containing images of students solving geometry problems. At certain points throughout the book, readers are referred to relevant video clips on the DVD. For the most part, these images, we believe, exemplify indicators of the geometric habits of mind. In addition, there are images that pertain to the importance in geometric problem solving of teacher questioning and of mathematical language and communication.

1

Geometric Habits of Mind

A Focus on Geometric Thinking

On an afternoon a few years ago, we were exploring geometric thinking with a group of mathematics coaches by using a set of relatively quick exercises. After each exercise, a few volunteers explained how they thought about it. From their reflections, we were trying to capture and describe the variety in thinking. One such exercise asked: "In two minutes or less, can you draw a quadrilateral that has two right angles but has no pair of parallel sides?" After a couple of minutes, three respondents put words to their thinking about the question.

Person A: I just started drawing, and pretty quickly realized that the two right angles couldn't be adjacent to each other, or else you'd have parallel sides. So they are opposite each other, and the other two angles, opposite each other, also have to add to 180 degrees. From putting two right angles opposite each other, it wasn't long before I had the other two angles and all four sides.

Person B: Right angles always suggest right triangles to me, so I drew one. Then I reflected it through the hypotenuse. I knew that, as long as the original triangle wasn't isosceles, the resulting quadrilateral fits the description (see Figure 1–1).

Person C: Believe it or not, when I hear "right angle," I think of circles—or, semicircles, actually. So, I drew a circle and diameter, picked a point A on

 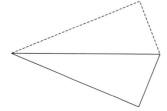

Figure 1–1

one side of the diameter, then a point B on the other side. I completed the right angles by connecting A and B to the ends of the diameter and there was the quadrilateral I wanted. Then I realized that I could get an infinite number of them by moving A along its semicircle, or by moving both A and B. I guess by doing that you'd get all the ones with a fixed diagonal connecting the non-right angles (see Figure 1–2).

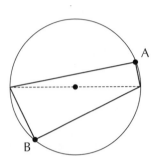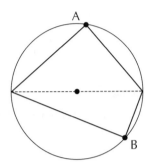

Figure 1–2

In revealing the rich variety of thinking that a relatively simple, though open, geometry challenge can produce, this incident is far from being atypical. There is something about asking people to visualize, construct, and reason in one, two, or three dimensions that seems to invite different ways of thinking. Of course, some ways are more productive than others. We have been working on a project, Fostering Geometric Thinking (FGT) in the Middle Grades,[1] funded by the National Science Foundation and dedicated to studying and describing productive geometric thinking in ways that can help teachers understand its development and foster students' geometric thinking. We place a high value on analyzing evidence of geometric thinking—both adults' and students'—to identify lines of thinking that make geometric problem solving successful, as well as common conceptual obstacles to productive geometric thinking. To explore lines of thinking, let's look at the preceding three examples.

Person A, after some experimentation with drawing and some visualizing, takes quick stock of what he's learned from experimenting, and then focuses mainly on the relationship that the angles in the desired figure must have with each other. This attention to, and reasoning about, relationships within and between geometric figures is fundamental to productive geometric thinking.

Person B also considers properties and relationships but adds some motion—reflecting the triangle through the hypotenuse. Because she knows something about what stays invariant under reflection (angles, for one thing), she's able to assure herself that she hasn't created a figure with four right angles by

[1]Fostering Geometric Thinking in the Middle Grades is a collaborative effort between Education Development Center and Horizon Research, Inc., spanning the years 2004–2008 (NSF EHR-0353409).

starting with a non–isosceles triangle. This consideration of the invariance of angles under reflection—however tacit it may have been for this coach—marks another key feature of productive geometric thinking.

Person C also made use of dynamics—points moving around the circle—to go beyond the problem's bounds and look for some general information. First, "How can I get more of them?" and then "How can I describe all of them?" This transfer of attention from one object to a whole class containing it is indicative of generalization—a core thinking process for mathematics and for geometry, in particular.

Later, we will return to the thinking of Persons A, B, and C to illustrate the evolving FGT conceptual framework based on geometric habits of mind.

The Geometric Habits of Mind Framework

Mathematical *habits of mind* are productive ways of thinking that support the learning and application of formal mathematics. A major premise of this book is that the learning of mathematics is as much about developing these mind habits as it is about understanding established results in the discipline called *mathematics*. Goldenberg, Cuoco, and Mark (1998) highlighted this notion of habits of mind, equating it with mathematical power:

> Mathematical power is best described by a set of *habits of mind*. People with mathematical power perform thought experiments; tinker with real and imagined machines; invent things; look for invariants (patterns); make reasonable conjectures; describe things both casually and formally (and play other language games); think about methods, strategies, algorithms, and processes; visualize things (even when the "things" are not inherently visual); seek to explain *why* things are as they see them; and argue passionately about intellectual phenomena. (39)

Building on earlier work around mathematical habits of mind (Driscoll 1999; Driscoll et al. 2001), FGT offers a framework highlighting productive mental habits geared specifically toward geometric thinking. Selecting Geometric Habits of Mind (GHOM) for our FGT framework has been an extended as well as iterative process, with revisions driven by several forces: conversations with project advisors (both mathematicians and mathematics educators) and with pilot and field-test teachers; examinations of the research literature on geometric thinking; and analyses of artifacts of student work on the problems that have been used during pilot and field tests. Throughout, we have been guided by four criteria:

- *Each GHOM should represent mathematically important thinking.* We aspire to have our framework reflect important lines of geometric thinking, particularly as they contribute to geometric problem solving.

- *Each GHOM should connect to helpful findings in the research literature on the learning of geometry and the development of geometric thinking.* We want to point teachers toward insights into the development of such thinking gained by researchers as well as insights into common hurdles faced by learners during that development.

- *Evidence of each GHOM should appear often in work with teachers and students.* We want to ensure that the lines of geometric thinking we choose to emphasize will show up, with some frequency, in the work of students in grades 5 through 10, even if the appearance may be unpolished and underdeveloped.

- *GHOMs should lend themselves to instructional use.* Our core interest is in helping teachers foster geometric thinking in and among their students. Each GHOM must point the way toward helpful instructional strategies— for example, productive questions to ask students or clues toward problem design and adaptation.

We have selected the following four GHOMs to constitute our framework, which we elaborate on in the next section:

- Reasoning with relationships
- Generalizing geometric ideas
- Investigating invariants
- Balancing exploration and reflection

Regarding the second criterion, we noticed when drawing from literature to support these choices, that many researchers' works on problem solving, advanced mathematical thinking, and cognitive processes have influenced our thinking. These include the following: Herbst (2006), in the context of geometric problem solving, has examined the development of what he calls *building reasoned conjectures*; Harel and Sowder (2005) have described reasoned inquiry through their Repeated Reasoning Principle, which involves proposing conjectures, investigating their viability, and supporting all conclusions with valid reasons; Bransford and colleagues (National Research Council 2005) emphasized the importance of explicit attention to the metacognitive in mathematics teaching and learning; Lesh, Lester, and Hjalmarson (2003) described the kinds of metacognitive processes associated with effective mathematical problem solving in grades K–12. All the researchers have helped to form our thinking about describing the development of geometric reasoning and reflection in grades 5 through 10.

Generalizing geometric ideas also has seemed important for us to attend to. Mitchelmore (2002) points out that "Generalizations . . . are at the core of school mathematics—numerical generalizations in algebra, spatial generalizations in geometry and measurement, and logical generalizations everywhere" (161). With Mitchelmore, we believe that school children are afforded too few opportunities to locate general results via investigation; rather, the norm tends to be that students are expected to learn and apply results obtained by others.

Barrett et al. (2006) have explored the development of understanding of linear measurement, and their account helped to highlight the role that attending to relationships among geometric objects, such as the congruence of opposite sides of rectangles, plays in geometric problem solving.

Also influencing our attention to the importance in geometric problem solving of seeing and using relationships was Duval's analysis of advanced geometric visualization, which accompanies construction and reasoning in his model of geometric thought. Duval (1998) observes that advanced geometers "see" not only the immediate impression of a geometric object but also the various configurations within objects that, as one establishes relationships among them, may serve as aids in problem solving. This process is exemplified in the following example.

→ *Noticing configurations:* In any trapezoid (quadrilateral with one pair of parallel sides), when the diagonals are drawn, two regions (the shaded regions) are created that may look very different but always have the same area (see Figure 1–3). This fact can seem mysterious or even remain unknown, until one notices and compares the two configurations in Figure 1–4.

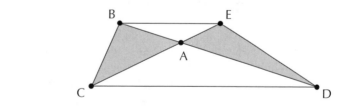

Figure 1–3

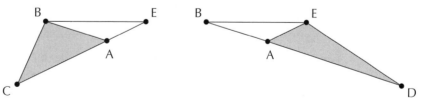

Figure 1–4

→ Each of these triangles has $\overline{BE}$ as base, and the height of the trapezoid as height. So, they have the same area. Since they also share △ABE, subtracting the area of it from the area of each triangle shows the equivalence of the areas of the two shaded regions.

In our planning, we also needed to consider tools that can help foster geometric thinking. In particular, the establishment of dynamic geometry tools in recent decades and the research springing from this new mode of geometry education have raised awareness of the value of recognizing both change and invariance in geometric contexts—see, for example, Hoyles and Jones (1998). Dynamic environments can dramatically highlight invariant features within an otherwise highly variable situation. This and other features have led some to argue that the new technology can and should substantially impact school geometry (Schwartz 1999).

GHOM Framework Descriptions

With the four criteria just listed as guides, we settled on four GHOMs. We describe each briefly next, with several prominent indicators of each. More comprehensive lists and descriptions of indicators appear later in the chapter.

Reasoning with Relationships   This is actively looking for relationships (e.g., congruence, similarity, parallelism) within and between geometric figures in one, two, and three dimensions, and thinking about how the relationships can help your understanding or problem solving. Internal questions (i.e., questions problem solvers ask themselves) include: "How are these figures alike?" "In how many ways are they alike?" "How are these figures different?" "What else here fits this description?" "What would I have to do to this object to make it like that object?" "What if I think about this relationship in a different dimension?"

- *Rationale:* To solve many geometry problems, it is advantageous to recognize how geometric objects in one, two, and three dimensions can be related to each other based on geometric properties. Often, the relationships can be exploited to arrive at exact problem solutions; without reasoning based on relationships, solvers are usually reduced to approximate solutions, at best.

- *Example:* In the opening example, Person A seemed to be reasoning with an awareness of relationships determined by parallel lines, and Person B seemed to be reasoning with symmetry relationships.

- *Indicators:* Basic indicators of this GHOM include the identification of figures presented in a problem and correct enumeration of their properties. More advanced indicators include relating multiple figures in a problem through proportional reasoning and reasoning through symmetry.

Generalizing Geometric Ideas   This is wanting to understand and describe the "always" and the "every" related to geometric phenomena. Internal questions include: "Does this happen in every case?" "Why would this happen in every case?" "Have I found *all the ones* that fit this description?" "Can I think of examples when this is not true; and, if so, should I then revise my generalization?" "Would this apply in other dimensions?"

- *Rationale: Generalizing*—shifting attention from a given set of objects to a larger set containing the given one—has been a driving force in the history of mathematics and, indirectly, in the history of science. Even within the narrower frame of school mathematics, it is important for young solvers of mathematics problems to learn that, quite often, it isn't adequate to find one solution, or even a finite number of solutions, to a posed problem.

- *Example:* Person C in the opening example used his knowledge of circles to create not only one quadrilateral but also to extend his awareness to an infinite class of examples.

- *Indicators:* The habit of generalizing can start to develop early when a solver uses one problem solution to generate another (e.g., through reflection in the plane), or when the solver intuits that he or she hasn't found all the solutions, perhaps because of not knowing how to identify them. More advanced geometric generalizers can generate all solutions and make a convincing argument as to why there are no more. Another more advanced indication of this GHOM is the habit of wondering what happens if a problem's context is changed (e.g., to a higher dimension).

Investigating Invariants   An *invariant* is something about a situation that stays the same, even as parts of the situation vary. This GHOM shows up, for example, in analyzing which attributes of a figure remain the same and which change when the figure is transformed in some way (e.g., through translations, reflections, rotations, dilations, dissections, combinations, or controlled distortions). Internal questions include: "How did that figure get from here to there?" "Is it possible to transform this figure so that it becomes that one?" "What changes? Why?" "What stays the same? Why?" "What happens to the figure if I keep applying the same transformations over and over again?"

- *Rationale:* In advanced mathematics, the idea of invariants under transformations is fundamental in distinguishing one kind of geometry from another. In many kinds of engineering, understanding what stays invariant under change is critical. Even for young mathematics learners, it is important to appreciate the role of mathematics in analyzing change, to understand that geometry is useful in analyzing change in space, and to realize that looking for what *doesn't* change under geometric transformation is often essential to geometric problem solving.

- *Example:* In the opening example, we suggested that Person B was implicitly capitalizing on the knowledge of what changes, what stays the same under reflections. A less subtle example of this GHOM may be the following. Knowing that a square's diagonals are perpendicular to each other, someone might do a thought experiment and imagine the square collapsing into flatter and flatter rhombi, and wondering what changes and what stays the same. Area changes as the shape varies but perimeter does not. And neither does the angle of intersection between the diagonals (see Figure 1–5).

 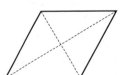 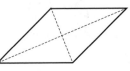 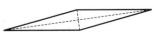

Figure 1–5

- *Indicators:* At a basic level, an indication of this GHOM appears when a solver decides to try a transformation of figures in a problem without being prompted to (as Person B did in the opening example), and considers what has changed and what has not changed. At more advanced levels, solvers naturally consider extreme cases for what is being asked by a problem (e.g., asking "If I let this vertex go out to infinity, will the area stay the same, and what happens to the perimeter?").

Balancing Exploration and Reflection
This is trying various ways to approach a problem and regularly stepping back to take stock. This balance of "What if . . ." with "What did I learn from trying that?" is representative of this habit of mind. Internal questions include: "What happens if I (draw a picture, add to/take apart this picture, work backward from the ending place, etc.)?" "What did that action tell me?" "How can my earlier attempts to solve the problem inform my approach now?" "What intermediate steps might help?" "What if I already had the solution . . . what would it look like?"

- *Rationale:* One characteristic of successful problem solvers is their metacognitive capacity to balance exploration with taking stock of the productivity of their explorations, then deducing where to take their exploration next. Habituating this appreciation of exploration in mathematics—often quite playful exploration—with metacognitive monitoring is the essence of this GHOM.

- *Example:* In the opening example, Person A's drawing, visualizing, and taking stock is representative of this GHOM.

- *Indicators:* Indications that this GHOM is developing include solvers drawing, playing, and/or exploring, with occasional (though maybe not consistent) stock-taking. Later indications can include approaching a problem by imagining what a final solution would look like, then reasoning backward;

or making what Herbst (2006) calls "reasoned conjectures" about solutions with strategies for testing the conjectures.

We make no claim that this four-point framework represents an exhaustive list of productive modes of geometric thought. Nor do we view the four habits of mind as mutually exclusive. Quite the opposite, a problem solver is likely to draw on several conceptual tools while approaching a problem, and it is quite possible that multiple GHOMs may be used to describe the same process. For example, a student who "discovers" pi by investigating the measurements of several circles has reasoned with the relationship between circumference and diameter, has found an invariant ratio between the two, and may even go so far as to generalize this relationship to all circles.

The third criterion for GHOM selection—*Evidence of each GHOM should appear often in work with teachers and students*—can be helpful in understanding the meaning of the GHOMs, so we cull from examples of teacher and student work helpful indicators of the different habits of mind. We hope that, in the end, these indicators will help teachers not only understand our meanings but also sharpen their thinking as they analyze students' work on geometric problems; we even invite teachers to add to the list of indicators.

GHOM Framework Examples

Generalizing Geometric Ideas   We can illustrate this strategy by considering the current list of GHOM *Generalizing geometric ideas* indicators. Simply put, mathematical generalization is "passing from the consideration of a given set of objects to that of a larger set, containing the given one" (Polya 1954, 12). In geometry, we are interested in generalized procedures ("Will your dissection method work for all parallelograms?"), generalized results ("As any two-dimensional figure's dimensions change by a factor of r, its area changes by a factor of r^2."), and generalized understanding of the properties of geometric figures ("Is that true of all trapezoids?"). Quite often, a problem asks for a locus of all points that fit certain conditions and the locus that fits can be infinite, either discrete (e.g., points on a lattice), continuous and bounded (e.g., points on a circle or line segment, points in the region bounded by a circle), or continuous and unbounded (e.g., points on a ray or straight line, points in an infinite region of the Cartesian plane).

Many of the FGT problems prompt thinking in terms of generalization by asking solvers to make a convincing argument that they have found all the solutions that fit the problem. In the course of tabulating responses, the following indicators of generalizing in people's efforts to respond were noted. This list is not intended to represent a linear progression. However, we observed that development of thinking moves from reliance on familiar examples to wider and more confident perspectives about what it means "to have them all."

Less Developed	Transitional	More Developed
<ul><li>Considers relevant special cases (e.g., right triangles, equilateral triangles)</li><li>Looks beyond special cases to some other examples that fit</li><li>Tries generating new cases by changing features in cases already identified (e.g., applies reflections, rotations)</li><li>Intuits that there are other solutions but doesn't know how to generate them (e.g., "There must be other points that work but their coordinates won't be nice numbers.")</li></ul>	<ul><li>Recognizes that given conditions work for an infinite set but considers only a discrete set (e.g., using points on a graph that have only integer coordinates)</li><li>Sees an infinite, continuously varying set of cases that work but limits the set (e.g., by looking only within a bounded space in the plane), or jumps to the wrong conclusion about the set (e.g., by representing the set with the wrong geometric shape)</li></ul>	<ul><li>Sees the entire set of solutions and can explain why there are no more.</li><li>Notices a rule that is universally true for a class of geometric figures (e.g., "If you double the size of all the sides of any polygon, you quadruple the area.")</li><li>Situates problems or rules in broader contexts (e.g., "I bet a similar thing happens in three dimensions—if you double the edges of a polyhedron, you make the volume go up eight times.")</li></ul>

Refer to the DVD for examples of students engaged in *Generalizing geometric ideas*. In Finding Area on a Coordinate Grid students demonstrate the third bulleted indicator and try generalizing new cases by changing features in cases already identified. In Finding Centers of Rotation (clip 1), while no student is able to achieve the eighth bulleted indicator, one of the students shows an understanding of its importance. As he and his group explore the problem, he repeatedly expresses concern that their rule, or method, may not be universally true for all pairs of line segments.

To see more of these indicators in a real context, consider a few solutions to a problem we have used with both teachers and students.

Perimeter Problem

Two vertices of a triangle are located at (4, 0) and (8, 0). The perimeter of the triangle is 12 units. What are all possible positions for the third vertex? How do you know you have them all?

Since we have the work samples of students across grades 5 through 10, along with teacher work in those grades, we have many examples of different ways to think about the problem; the range of responses covers all the bullets in the preceding indicator list.

In particular, at the level of greatest generalization, many problem solvers recognized that the possible positions lie on and constitute an ellipse with foci (4, 0) and (8, 0), and do so with a variety of techniques (e.g., using a piece of string pinned at the two points) and reasoning (e.g., representing the set with the appropriate equations in x and y). Examples of indicators at other levels of generalizing are plentiful.

Less Developed Examples   First bullet—considers relevant special cases—responses generally resemble the representation we have constructed from multiple examples of work that is shown in Figure 1–6. In this sample, there also appears to be an indication of the third bullet—tries generating new cases—in that we can infer that the solvers expanded the original set of 3 triangles to 6 by reflecting through the x-axis.

Transitional Examples   The third and, arguably, the fourth bullet—recognizes that given conditions work—indicators are represented in the work of solvers who recognized that the lengths of the other two sides must add to 8; then they use that fact to try to generate new examples. Several responses we have seen sound like this: "Will all values between 1 and 8 work, as long as they add up to 8? Or is there a range in which it still will be a triangle? . . . In other words, would 0.25 and 7.75 still make a triangle with 4? No, the short side couldn't connect with the third vertex. . . . How can I possibly find them all? How do I know what the angles are without measuring?" (By the way, the seeming absence, in this kind of response, of knowledge about the Triangle Inequality underscores the importance of the relationship among sides it represents, and reinforces our desire to attend to the GHOM, *Reasoning with relationships*.)

FIGURE 1–6

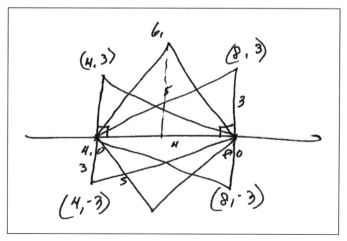

More Developed Examples Representative of the third and sixth bullets are the samples in which the solvers write statements such as the following (a compilation of samples): "Find the first point by approximation and then reflect it over the *x*-axis. Now I have 2 points. Find another point and then reflect it over the *x*-axis. Continue this process until I notice that my points are forming a circle." These solvers arrived at a faulty conclusion (conjecturing circular shape, not elliptical); however, in seeing that the final set of points is symmetric with respect to the *x*-axis, they are also exemplifying one of the indicators we are paying attention to for the GHOM, *Balancing exploration and reflection*—"describes what the final state would look like (e.g., in order to see whether there is any way to reason backward)."

As teachers become more adept at recognizing the different GHOM indicators, we expect that they will see lines of potential for which their questions, challenges, and other instructional moves can foster student geometric thinking. For example, the listed *Generalizing geometric ideas* indicators show gaps of thinking defined by limited attention to whole-number solution sets, or to finite solution sets, or to discrete instead of continuous solution sets. With these gaps in mind when attending to their students' geometric thinking, teachers can use classroom questioning to assess the extent to which gaps exist and to advance student thinking across the gaps. Furthermore, guiding students to think in greater generality about objects can influence teachers' selection and adaptation of geometry problems for students to engage with.

Similarly, we believe that greater acuity when it comes to the other GHOMs can help teachers foster their students' geometric thinking. For example, taking a cue from samples in the preceding examples, teachers can ask questions like these: "To make a triangle, what relationship do three segments need to have with each other?" (*Reasoning with relationships*); and "Suppose you had the set of points you are looking for. Is there anything you can say for sure about the shape of that set?" (*Investigating invariants and balancing exploration and reflection*). The next sections briefly look at the other GHOM indicator lists.

Reasoning with Relationships

In our examination of work on problems that elicit thinking about geometric relationships, we have noted the following GHOM indicators, which divide according to whether the focus is on comparing separate figures or analyzing what the relevant constituent parts of a single figure are. The list also includes use of special kinds of reasoning skills.

Focused on multiple figures

- Compares two geometric figures by enumerating some properties they have in common (which may or may not be relevant to the problem)

- Compares two geometric figures by enumerating all properties they have in common (relevant to the problem), and why

- Contrasts two geometric figures by noting properties they do not have in common

- Compares figures by considering relationships for their one-dimensional, two-dimensional, or three-dimensional components (e.g., relates the side lengths of similar triangles, as well as the areas)

Focused on the pieces in a single figure

- Notices and relates configurations within a geometric figure (e.g., looks at a geometric puzzle and sees that a subset of pieces form a rectangle)

- Constructs configurations within a geometric figure (e.g., connects vertices in a polygon to divide it into a set of triangles)

- Relates two geometric figures by noticing they can be seen as parts of a single geometric figure (e.g., "If I extend these two line segments, they will become two of the sides of a rectangle"; "If I put these two pieces together, they form a square.")

Use of special reasoning skills

- Reasons proportionally about two or more geometric figures (e.g., "One of these triangles has sides that are 1.5 times as long as the sides of the other triangle. From that I can figure out the relationship between the areas of the two.")

- Uses symmetry to relate geometric figures (e.g., "The altitude of this isosceles triangle divides the triangle into two triangles, one the mirror image of the other.")

Refer to the DVD for examples of students engaged in *Reasoning with relationships*. In the Folding to Construct Shapes clip students demonstrate the first bulleted indicator, comparing the properties of parallel lines, perpendicular lines, and squares. In Comparing Triangles a group of students exhibit the fourth bulleted indicator as they relate rectangles in terms of area and length. Students notice and relate configurations within a geometric figure, the fifth bulleted indicator, in the Finding Sides of Triangles clip as they rediscover the Triangle Inequality. The final video clip for the *Reasoning with relationships* GHOM, Finding Centers of Rotation (clip 1), shows students engaged in the seventh bulleted indicator. The students in this clip relate pairs of line segments in ways that allow them to be seen as part of a single geometric figure.

Consider the following challenge and track your thinking as you answer it.

In the rectangle in Figure 1–7, with lines parallel to the rectangle sides drawn through E on a diagonal, can you find a relationship between the two shaded rectangles?

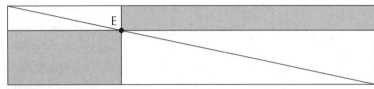

Figure 1–7

→ After you think about it, go back to the preceding indicator list to see whether you can connect your thinking to one or more of the indicators.

Investigating Invariants   Suppose this question was added to the previous challenge: *Does the relationship change if E is moved along the diagonal?* That pertains to investigating invariants—What stays the same? What changes? The indicators of this GHOM, as accumulated from example work, seem to divide along the lines of thinking dynamically and checking evidence of the effects of transformations—the two sides of the coin of investigating invariants.

Dynamic thinking

- Thinks dynamically about a static case (e.g., "I wonder whether it will be easier to figure out the area of this figure if I cut it up and move the pieces around?")

- Wonders about what changes, what stays the same when a transformation is applied (e.g., "When I rotate a line segment around this point, what happens to the midpoint—it stays in the middle, right?")

- Generates a number of cases of transformation effects and looks for commonalities (e.g., "We've dilated this triangle x2, x3, x(0.5) and recorded what's changed and what hasn't.")

- Thinks about the effects of moving a point or figure continuously and predicts occurrences in between one point and another (e.g., "Here's a triangle with perimeter 12 and area 6, and another triangle with perimeter 12 and area 4. There must be a triangle with perimeter 12 and area 5 somewhere in between.")

- Considers limit cases and extreme cases under transformations (e.g., "What happens to the diagonals' intersection point as this figure collapses to a line segment?"; "As the top vertex of this triangle moves around a circle, I wonder at which point the triangle's area is largest?")

Checking evidence of effects

- Intuits that not everything is changing as a transformation is applied (e.g., "Each time we dilated one of these triangles, we got one that seemed to be like the one we started with—just bigger.")

- Notices that the same effect appears to happen each time a particular type of transformation is applied, and says so (e.g., "Each time we dilated one of these triangles, the angles seemed to stay the same.")

- Notices invariants when a transformation is applied, and explains why they are invariants (e.g., "When you reflect a triangle through a line, you get a triangle that's congruent. That's because reflecting is like paper-folding, and you don't change the size or shape of figures when you move them by folding paper.")

Refer to the DVD for examples of students engaged in *Investigating invariants*. In Dilating Triangles (clip 1) students demonstrate the second bulleted indicator as they consider what stays the same and what changes during a dilation transformation. In Finding Centers of Rotation (clip 2) students engage in the fifth bulleted indicator as they notice the same effect appears to happen each time a line segment is rotated around its center of rotation.

Several of these bulleted indicators appeared when a student was asked what happens when you have a triangle with vertices at (5, 2), (1, 1), and (1, 5) and the vertex at (5, 2) is allowed to travel along the vertical line $x = 5$. Using dynamic software, she created a series of images like those in Figure 1–8.

As she kept up this change process, she remarked that "the area stays the same because the base and height don't change, but the perimeter keeps growing larger and larger." In this student's remark are several of the *Investigating invariants* indicators, particularly those that pertain to checking evidence.

Balancing Exploration and Reflection
Negative cases made this habit of mind appear important. That is, we observed several videotaped cases of students energetically exploring a problem (e.g., a geometric puzzle problem) yet rarely, if ever, stopping to take stock of why they were trying particular moves or whether the moves were productive in any way. So, the indicators here separate into the two sides of the balance: focused on exploration moves and focused on the bigger picture. Both are crucial, in balance.

FIGURE 1–8

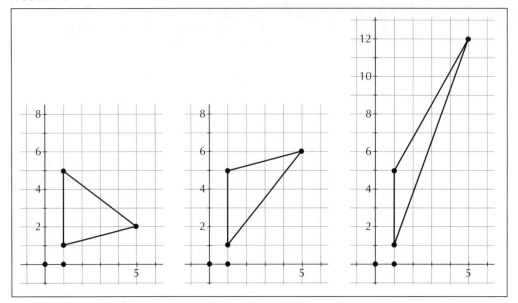

Exploration in foreground

- Draws, plays, and/or explores through intuition or guessing (e.g., "This doesn't seem to work. Let's try something different . . .")

- Draws, plays, and/or explores with some stock-taking (e.g., "Did that move do any good?")

- Tries familiar strategies (e.g., "What have I tried before?")

- Changes or considers changing some feature of a situation, condition, or geometric figure (e.g., "What if I connected these two points instead of those two?")

End goals in foreground

- Returns periodically to the big picture as a touchstone of progress (e.g., "Now, how does that connect to what we're supposed to find?")

- Identifies intermediate steps that can help get to the goal (e.g., "We know how to make a rectangle from a parallelogram, so if we can make a parallelogram out of this figure, we'll have it.")

- Describes what the final state would look like (e.g., to see whether there is any way to reason backward—"Well, I know the final set of points will be symmetric about the y-axis, so what might that shape look like?")

22 ▪ ▪ ▪ *Geometric Habits of Mind*

- Makes reasoned conjectures about solutions, creating ways to test the conjectures (e.g., "All the points that work will be symmetric about the *y*-axis. I think that means it will be a circle. To test that, we need to decide where the center of that circle would be, and then draw the circle and find out whether points on it work.")

Refer to the DVD for examples of students engaged in *Balancing exploration and reflection*. In Puzzling with Polygons, students demonstrate the first bulleted indicator, experimenting with different shape combinations. Students engage in the fifth bulleted indicator in Investigating Area by Folding Paper, periodically returning to the big picture to assess how close they are to finding the target square. The final video clip for the *Balancing exploration and reflection* GHOM, Dissecting Shapes (clip 1), shows students engaged in the sixth bulleted indicator. After some time exploring the problem, the students discover that a successful dissection of the parallelogram will have to produce right angles.

One of the problems we have used asks for solvers to develop three different ways to calculate the area of a set of polygons on a grid, including the irregular pentagon shown in Figure 1–9.

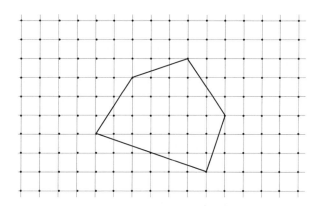

Figure 1–9

A group of math coaches, who were helping us think about this problem, took this a step beyond three ways, and explored how many different ways they could solve the problem. They came up with quite a few. Figure 1–10 displays a method reported by one small group: dissection of the figure and reconstitution as a square.

As they reported it, their thinking proceeded along lines similar to: "We figured the area of the pentagon was 25 square units by cutting it up into little triangles. Then we thought 'Well, that is the area of a 5 × 5 square. Let's try to make that square out of the pentagon.' Then we started cutting and rotating and

FIGURE 1–10

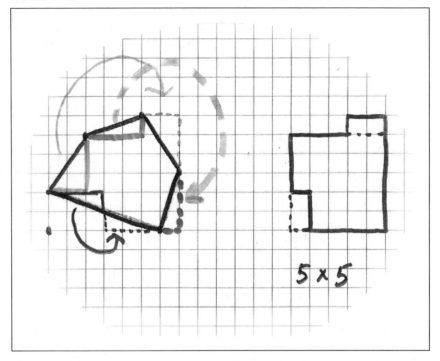

matching pieces." A couple of things occurred to us when the coaches shared this.

First, it seemed a very instructive example of the indicator of *Balancing exploration and reflection*—"describes what the final state would look like." Second, it illustrates the value of a problem-solving strategy George Polya advocated decades ago (Polya 1945). "Looking Back," as he called it, means not only asking, "Did I do all that the problem asked?" but also wondering, "Are there other ways I could have solved it?" Doing all that a problem requires is essential to mathematics achievement; however, it is in asking the latter question that productive mathematical thinking is really sharpened.

2 *Geometric Relationships*

Introduction

In its five mathematical essays on Change, Dimension, Quantity, Shape, and Uncertainty, the influential 1990 book *On the Shoulders of Giants* (Steen 1990) made the case that mathematics is the language and science of patterns in each of these topic areas and beyond. Pattern-seeking is valuable to a large extent because it can reveal relationships that in turn can serve mathematical problem solving. For example, becoming aware that there is a constant–proportion relationship between corresponding sides of similar triangles has value in its own right, but the value grows immensely when that relationship is used to solve problems.

Relationships that have particular importance in the school mathematics of grades 5 through 9 are the numerical relationships studied in algebra and the spatial relationships studied in geometry. This chapter emphasizes the latter and also enumerates the similarities and differences between the two kinds of relationships. Then, harking back to the Sir Michael Atiyah quote that leads off the Introduction, it makes the case that we want students to be adept at using both kinds of reasoning with relationships in their problem solving. Let's start with several examples.

Relationships Example 1

Arguably, the way mathematics problems are framed can make it challenging for algebraic and geometric reasoning to act in concert in a problem solver's brain. That is, if a problem asks for a numeric or quantitative outcome, it is often inviting and comfortable to think algebraically. Similarly, if the desired outcome has to do with shape, location, and so on of objects in space, then it is inviting and comfortable to think geometrically. In each case, the solver is likely to pay attention to different aspects of the problem.

Several years ago, in a session on algebraic thinking, a group of middle-grades teachers worked on The Staircase Problem:

The Staircase Problem

Staircase 1 has 1 block, Staircase 2 has 1 + 2 = 3 blocks, Staircase 3 has 1 + 2 + 3 = 6 blocks, Staircase 4 has 1 + 2 + 3 + 4 = 10 blocks, and so on. How many blocks are in Staircase N?

Nearly all the teachers focused on the sequence of numbers and compiled tables like the one shown in Figure 2–1.

Nth staircase	# of blocks
1	1
2	3
3	6
4	10
5	15
.	.
.	.

Figure 2–1

At this point, the teachers tried various moves aimed at revealing numerical patterns, such as taking successive differences in the right column, but generally they made no progress and were stuck. At the edge of the group, working by himself, a teacher was drawing pictures of each successive staircase on graph paper. After ten minutes or so, he let out, "Aha!" Later he reported his insight: Each staircase, while itself an irregular geometric figure, had a clear relationship with a very regular and familiar geometric figure, the square. See Figure 2–2 for an illustration of that relationship as demonstrated for Staircase 3.

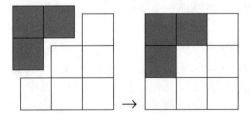

Figure 2–2

Now he could see that the square was composed of a staircase and the previous staircase, and he was left to translate this geometric relationship into a numerical relationship involving N: "Let's see. If I subtract N, the number of *blocks* in the diagonal, from N^2, I get two versions of the previous staircase. That means that the $(N-1)$th staircase has $(N^2 - N)/2 = N(N-1)/2$ blocks in it. So, the Nth staircase has $(N+1)N/2$ blocks in it."

The other teachers, of course, were also looking for a relationship—a numerical relationship—and most eventually succeeded by adding a column to their table that let them compute the "difference of differences," which they realized was constant. From there, they reasoned that they had a quadratic relationship, and followed through to the expression $N(N+1)/2$ as defining the numerical relationship between N and the number of blocks in the Nth staircase.

We do not offer this story to imply that the lone teacher's way of thinking was superior. Neither way of thinking was necessarily "better" than the other; indeed, each provided its own set of insights into the problem. Rather, we offer the story because what the teacher did was significant: to step away from the number–algebra mind-set of his colleagues and ask: "What can the geometric relationships tell me?"

From a fostering geometric thinking (FGT) perspective, we would say that the teacher was making use of the geometric habits of mind (GHOM) *Reasoning with relationships* indicator between geometric figures in a context where the quantitative was emphasized more than the spatial. His thinking seemed to be consistent with the GHOM indicator listed in Chapter 1, "relates two geometric figures by noticing they can be seen as parts of a single geometric figure" (see page 19).

You can try to employ the same GHOM on a different problem:

Which numbers can be expressed as the difference of two perfect squares? For example, $3 = 4 - 1$, $9 = 25 - 16$, and so on.

→ Think about this problem for five minutes or so, then do a quick review of how you are thinking about it. Now read what follows.

The problem invites thinking in terms of numerical relationships. If you make a table and start to gather data, you can see at least one conjecture taking shape: "Any odd number can be expressed as the difference of two consecutive perfect squares."

To test whether this conjecture is on target, it is perfectly fine to apply algebraic reasoning to the expression $(n+1)^2 - n^2$—the general difference of two consecutive perfect squares. However, like the lone teacher discussed before, think in terms of the geometric meaning of "perfect squares," and ask yourself, "What can geometric relationships tell me?"

- Can they tell you whether the conjecture is true?
- Can they help you determine whether even numbers can be expressed as the difference of perfect squares?

Once you follow through with geometric reasoning, return to the problem and apply reasoning that is more algebraic than geometric.

- What insights about the problem did geometric reasoning provide?
- What insights about the problem did algebraic reasoning provide?

Relationships Example 2

In our field test of the Fostering Geometric Thinking Toolkit materials, we used a problem that included the following challenge.

Comparing Triangles

Take a rectangular piece of paper and fold it so that corner A folds to A' somewhere along side CD, as can be seen in the picture in Figure 2–3. There are three triangles showing from your fold (one hidden under the fold). They are all right triangles. What else do you notice about these triangles?

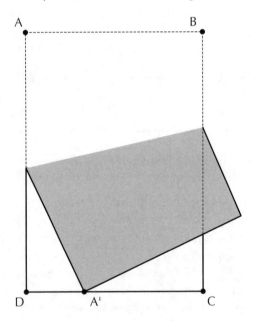

Figure 2–3

→ Take a little time and think about what the problem is asking, and be aware of your geometric reasoning as you answer the question it poses.

In solving the problem, it is likely you employed the GHOM *Reasoning with relationships*—in particular, the relationships between each pair of triangles. As in most other geometric problems, thinking also is guided by what the solver notices or pays attention to in the geometric figures featured in a problem. For example, one could fold, then unfold, and use the fold line (dotted in the diagram in Figure 2–4) as a line of symmetry, and track where the hidden triangle would be under the reflection (upper right corner). One also might pay attention to the two quadrilaterals (one on each side of the dotted fold line).

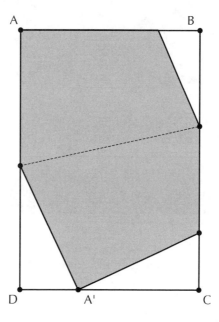

Figure 2–4

Figure 2–5 shows part of the newsprint presentation on the problem by a group of teachers who did just that.

Paying attention to the two quadrilaterals formed in the fold, the teachers then attended to the symmetry relationship between the two quadrilaterals, with the fold as a line of symmetry. Reasoning with this symmetry relationship, along with the relationships between transversals and parallel lines, they were able to identify and color-code angles, and so concluded that triangles 1, 2, and 3 are similar.

In their thinking, the teachers didn't attend to quantities represented in the problem at all. This raises the question: "What quantitative relationships might one wonder about?" Consider what three students of an FGT field-test teacher did. The teacher divided her students into small groups, handed them a variety of rectangular sheets of paper, told them to explore the problem, then to put their thoughts, conjectures, and so forth on newsprint. This particular trio of

FIGURE 2–5

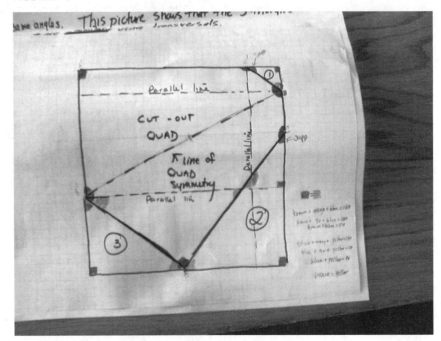

students decided to explore what happens when the original sheet of paper is a square. They then asked the question: "Is there a location of A′ where all three of the triangles are isosceles?"

Using a ruler to measure, they tried different-sized squares and began to notice a pattern. (We think this was a good example of *Sustaining Reasoned Exploration*.) The particular relationship they attended to was the ratio of the length of segment DA′ to the length of side DC. As evidenced in our replica of their newsprint presentation in Figure 2–6, their calculations kept showing the relationship to be about 0.4. They were left with the conjecture—"It's always going to be 0.4 for squares."—that invited further exploration; in our GHOM language, they were *Investigating invariants*.

The ratio is actually $1/(\sqrt{2} + 1) = \sqrt{2} - 1$, which is approximately 0.414. So, the students were onto something. Your task is twofold: convince yourself that this is the exact ratio, and then outline a way in which you might help students understand how this invariant arises.

The Comparing Triangles video clip demonstrates how a group of students explored an extended version of this problem.

FIGURE 2–6

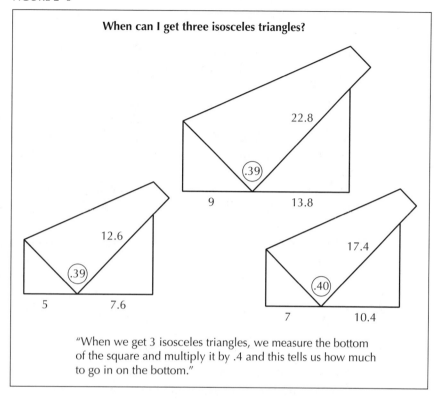

When can I get three isosceles triangles?

22.8

.39

9   13.8

12.6

.39

5   7.6

17.4

.40

7   10.4

"When we get 3 isosceles triangles, we measure the bottom of the square and multiply it by .4 and this tells us how much to go in on the bottom."

Reasoning About Geometric Relationships: Research Summary

In this book we place a high value on the Geometric Habit of Mind *Reasoning with relationships*, which raises questions about students' capacities, in middle grades and beyond, both to understand geometric relationships and to reason about them. This section considers some factors that can influence students' capacities. Here we incorporate much of the research that has built on the pioneering work of the van Hieles, beginning in the 1950s (Fuys, Geddes, and Tischler 1988). The van Hiele model of thinking in geometry proposed five levels of thinking, starting at a level of thinking that is mostly visual and progressing to a level where students can construct mathematical proofs and compare and contrast different geometric systems.

For the purposes of this book, we start at the beginning of the middle-grades experience. Most students enter the middle grades with a limited understanding of geometric figures and their properties. While most students are able to identify examples of triangles, rectangles, and other polygons, many exemplars of these shapes still escape their detection (Carroll 1998). At the start of middle school, students' concepts of geometric figures are predominantly image-based. Despite memorizing verbal definitions, such as, "A rectangle is a four-sided figure with four right angles," students do not immediately incorporate lists of shape properties into their concepts of shapes. This is apparent in comments students make suggesting given figures are not particular shapes simply because they do not *look like* that shape (Clements 2003). Visually salient, yet unimportant, characteristics (e.g., orientation) often preclude students from recognizing instances of a particular shape (Clements and Battista 1992).

Concept formation generally, but in geometry particularly, is a process that evolves gradually and through struggle. As Vygotsky (1986) noted:

> Concept formation is a creative, not a mechanical passive process; . . . a concept emerges and takes shape in the course of a complex operation aimed at the solution of some problem. . . . memorizing words and connecting them with objects does not in itself lead to concept formation. (99)

Progression of Thinking About Relationships

A fully formed shape concept will eventually contain two kinds of information: visual exemplars and a set of critical properties (Hershkowitz 1989). Students progress through three ways of thinking as they move toward well-developed concepts. They first go through a stage where they reason based on the holistic appearance of a single prototypical image meant to represent the concept. Then, during the next two stages, attention shifts away from holistic appearance as students become more aware of geometric properties. Students experience a period where they overgeneralize properties from their prototype image such that both critical and noncritical properties are used as criteria. They then settle in on the properties critical to a shape's existence.

Stage 1: Students' shape concept consists of the <u>appearance of a single prototype</u>   When students are reasoning based on the holistic appearance of a single prototype, the image is perceived as a perfect example of the concept, and potential instances of a concept are judged according to their likeness to this representation. A student who has created the prototype similar to the one shown in Figure 2–7 is likely to comment: "A, B, and D aren't quadrilaterals because they don't look like quadrilaterals."

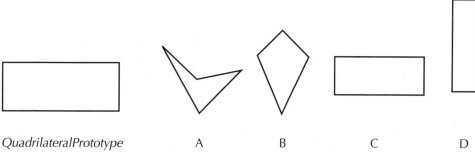

QuadrilateralPrototype   A   B   C   D

Figure 2–7

Educational researchers often target textbooks as the source of this prototype fixation, arguing that texts favor certain shape exemplars, depicting most images in a perfectly horizontal orientation with equivalent side lengths and angles when the definition allows. In fact, textbooks do favor typical shape representations just like students do with their prototypes (Clements 2003). However, it is not at all clear that texts are the cause of students' affinity for particular orientations and configurations. There is evidence to suggest that even in the absence of visual exemplars, one's visual perception system creates a visual prototype, and that prototypes are similar from individual to individual because of the salience of certain features—for example, orientation and equal line segments are more salient to our visual system.

In one study, when both students and teachers were presented verbal definitions for an invented shape concept and asked to draw the shape, the majority drew similar images (Hershkowitz 1989). For example, in response to reading "A bitrian is a geometric shape consisting of two triangles having a common vertex," most students and teachers drew one of the images shown in Figure 2–8. Very few students or teachers drew any of the images in Figure 2–9, all of which fit the definition of a bitrian.

Figure 2–8

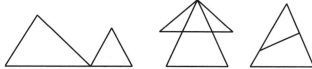

Figure 2–9

More students and teachers produced the first three than the second three, suggesting that even in the absence of visual exemplars, commonalities in the way the human perceptual system works leads most people to generate similar prototypes. Certain visual properties are more salient than others, and they register spontaneously, even when a verbal definition fails to reference them.

Finally, to demonstrate that this phenomenon is not particular to the bitrian, a similar result was found when students and teachers were asked to draw a biquad. The *biquad* was defined as "a geometric shape consisting of two quadrilaterals having a common side." Again, no additional information was given yet the majority of participants produced drawings similar to the two in Figure 2–10. Very few drew figures like the biquads shown in Figure 2–11.

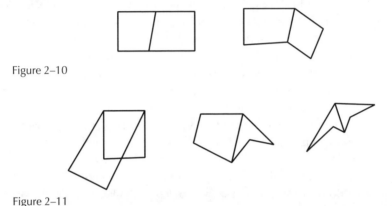

Figure 2–10

Figure 2–11

Stage 2: Students' shape concept consists of a single prototype and its properties

As students participate in activities allowing them to investigate the geometric properties of shapes, they move beyond a reliance on visual appearance and begin to analyze properties. Like visually based reasoning, however, first attempts at property-based reasoning still rely on the prototype as a frame of reference. Because the prototype is a specific example of the shape concept, it has additional properties that are not critical to the concept.

Students at this stage of concept development overgeneralize the prototype's properties and reason based on both critical and noncritical properties. When engaged in this type of reasoning, students identify right and isosceles triangles with horizontal bases as triangles more often than other triangles (Clements 2003); and when asked to differentiate between a square and rectangle, they comment: "The length of a square is more short than the rectangle" or "A rectangle is a four-sided shape but it is longer" (Monaghan 2000).

Often, even when students have a definition that lists the shape's critical properties, the prototype they create is so powerful that they use it as the frame of reference, generalizing concept properties from the prototype rather than from the definition. When students and teachers who had been introduced to the bitrian and biquad were presented with an array of figures and asked to identify all the examples of the two shapes, the majority of the participants did not recognize a number of exemplars. They were provided with verbal definitions detailing the shapes' critical properties, yet they reasoned from their prototypes (Hershkowitz 1989).

Stage 3: Students' shape concept consists of many exemplars and a set of critical properties

Most middle school students reason at the first two stages of concept development (Carroll 1998). However, as students continue to engage in geometric tasks, two things occur: (1) the number of exemplars associated with a concept increases to include images beyond the single prototype, and (2) students become aware of properties critical to defining a given shape. All the exemplars are mathematically equivalent in the sense that they all satisfy the set of critical properties. However, the exemplars differ visually from one another in that each has its own specific geometric properties that make it unique. The geometric properties common to all exemplars become the critical properties—those necessary and sufficient to defining this concept.

Individuals with a fully developed concept can identify and produce a variety of typical and atypical concept examples. A student at this level would not only recognize that shapes A, B, and C are all right triangles, but he or she also would be able to cite the critical properties of right triangles that all three of them share—they contain three sides and a right angle (see Figure 2–12). The students have a broadened sense of a right triangle. Orientation and side lengths are not important criteria for an instance of this concept.

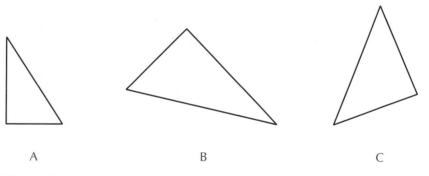

A   B   C

Figure 2–12

An important message conveyed in the van Hiele model still pertains: progress through stages of concept development in geometry is related to education not maturation. Hence, throughout this book we advocate for all students to receive a steady diet of challenging problems and teacher questions to assess their thinking and foster geometric reasoning. The value of such a diet is particularly high when it comes to the development of understanding of geometric properties, as well as relationships based on those properties. As students progress through the middle grades, and confront questions that push on concept differentiation (e.g., "What is the difference between a rectangle and a square?") and relationships between figures (e.g., "Why are all squares also rectangles but all rectangles are not squares?"), they become more and more aware of the inadequacy of their image-based concepts.

The Role of Language

Another conclusion from the work of the van Hieles, and of those who have followed in their footsteps, pertains to the role of language in teaching geometry: each stage of concept development has its own language, so two students at different stages may have trouble communicating with each other. Hence, teachers need to be alert to their students' use of language in geometry.

While teachers boost middle-graders' geometric reasoning and conceptual understanding, there is a concomitant need to help them develop their language so that it is more precise and mathematical. We have seen instances where the word *same* has been used to describe the relationship between two congruent figures in one instance and two similar figures in another. Consider the following exchange among three eighth-grade girls who have just completed the first part of a problem asking them whether they can figure out a way to cut up a given parallelogram and reconfigure all the cut pieces to make a rectangle. They were asked whether their method generalizes to all parallelograms.

Student 1: (*reads from paper*) "Will your method allow you to transform any parallelogram into a rectangle? Explain." So, get a marker. If there was like a small parallelogram, if we cut it, do you think we could make a rectangle with it?

Student 3: If we cut it like that (*pointing and tracing onto paper*) wouldn't it?

Student 1: Or, we could use the same strategy.

Student 2: Try cutting another parallelogram.

Student 1: (*draws and cuts a parallelogram that is a smaller, mathematically similar version of the one they had worked on*) This is what we did before right?

Other two students: Mm hmm . . .

Student 1: Here's a square (*pointing to a rectangle within the parallelogram*) and then . . . (*lines up cut-out shape onto paper*), yeah, you could do it with any parallelogram.

Student 2: But the point is, that was the same one as that (*pointing at shapes*) and we have to try making different ones to see if it will get into a rectangle.

Student 1: But isn't this shape, wait, I don't get what you're saying. Isn't this a parallelogram? This shape (*pointing to paper*).

Student 2: Yeah it is, but there are more parallelograms we could try to make go into a rectangle.

Student 1: What other ones? (*Student 2 doesn't answer and looks at her paper.*)

Student 1: I think like, that this is just the shape . . . You know how there's square, and rectangle and then there's a triangle. I think that is just a parallelogram. I think that how you said before that, if you cut the two right angles on the sides then you can make a rectangle.

Student 2: So the answer would be "yes," right?

In addition to the transcript provided here, this exchange is represented in Dissecting Shapes (clip 1) on the DVD.

There are several important things to observe in this exchange. First, it suggests that, even in eighth grade, students still can have limited conceptions of geometric figures. At least this is one inference to draw from the statement, "You know how there's square, and rectangle and then there's a triangle. I think that is just a parallelogram." (One of our FGT advisors offered another possible inference: the phrase "any parallelogram" in the problem statement didn't mean "all parallelograms" to the student.)

Second, it may underscore the difficulty in communication that can arise for students at two different stages (i.e., Student 1 and Student 2). Finally, it underscores the value of students' learning to make mathematical distinctions using correct mathematical language. It appears that Student 2 sees the *similarity* of the parallelogram that Student 1 decides to use as a test case. Student 2 also sees that the concept "parallelogram" encompasses a wide range of shapes, but she appears unable to express her insights in words and/or examples.

The issue of helping students develop a sharp accuracy in their use of mathematical language is more than a matter of emphasizing definition and vocabulary. Those are key elements, but it is also important to engage students at a reasoning level. We have found it valuable to keep a key question to ask in mind when the relationship between two figures is unclear, a question that also helps students develop the *Investigating invariants* GHOM:

→ *What is the same, and what is different, between those two?* "You've just cut up a parallelogram and made a rectangle from the pieces. What has stayed the same in this transition, and what is different? You said that those two figures are 'the same,' but one is bigger than the other. What is the same, and what is different?"

As students respond to questions like these, expressing their reasoning, teachers can be listening for opportunities to correct or extend their use of mathematical language. Opportunities to build academic language in the context of engaging in mathematical challenges are important for all students in middle grades and especially important for English learners. This comes across vividly in reports on a study of a fifth-grade teacher whose pseudonym is Sarah (Chval and Khisty 2001; Khisty and Chval 2002).

At the time of the study, Sarah was teaching in a school that is nearly 100 percent Latino in one of the poorest neighborhoods in a large urban school district. She was the focus of the research because of her consistent track record of significantly raising the mathematics achievement of her students. In tracing the roots of this success, the researchers documented her consistent use of writing assignments and classroom discourse related to challenging mathematics problems. Sarah used the occasions to clarify—not simplify—mathematical language.

Consider the following brief interaction between Sarah and her students (Chval and Khisty 2001, 23). A similar exchange is recorded in Khisty and Chval (2002, 8). It is the first week of school for these fifth graders, and they have been engaged in a challenging geometry problem. (The word *congruent* was introduced in the full-class discussion.)

Sarah: Look at that word everyone. *Congruent*. What does that mean?
Student: Like another copy.
Sarah: An exact copy. Because here, look, here is the circle. Is this circle congruent to that circle?
Chorus: No.
Sarah: No, they're not exact copies. They're similar. They're both circles, but they're not exact copies.

Fostering GHOMs Through Problems

Given this chapter's topic, one might expect that the problems featured here foster *Reasoning with relationships*. Early in the chapter, the Comparing Triangles problem fostered thinking about and reasoning with similarity relationships.

Problem 1

Rich problems can tap other GHOMs, as well. For example, we have found paper-folding problems to be in that category. One that we have used follows.

Folding to Construct Shapes

Use a pen or marker, a straightedge (if you use a ruler as your straightedge do not measure!), and patty paper to complete the constructions described in the problems here. You can fold the patty paper to create creases, and since it is see-through paper, you can use the folds to construct geometric objects.

1. Draw a line segment on the patty paper, making sure the line segment is not parallel to the edges of the paper.
   a. Construct a line segment that is a perpendicular bisector to your original segment.
      i. Describe your construction method.

    ii. How do you know your new line segment is a perpendicular bisector?

  b. Construct a line segment that is parallel to your original segment.

    i. Describe your construction method.

    ii. How do you know your new line segment is parallel to your original segment?

2. For each of the following, start with a freshly drawn segment on a clean piece of patty paper, then construct the shape.

  a. A square, with your segment as one of its sides

    i. Describe your construction method in pictures (a fold could be represented by a dotted line ⟋) and words.

    ii. Were there methods you tried that didn't work? What were those methods?

    iii. What are the properties of a square? How do you know your shape has each of the properties?

  b. An isosceles triangle, with your segment as one of the two equal sides

  c. An isosceles triangle, with your segment as the base

  d. An equilateral triangle, with your segment as one of its sides

  e. Choose one of the triangles you just constructed and describe your construction method in pictures and words.

DVD

The Folding to Construct Shapes video clip demonstrates how a group of students explored parts 1b and 2a of this problem.

Discussion   Among geometric relationships, symmetry, similarity, and congruence often provide quick routes to problem solving. This paper-folding problem is offered to students (and to teachers) to help them hone their reasoning with those relationships. Occasionally, one can see the power such experiences can have. Here is one student's narrative of how he reasoned about part 1a of the problem—folding to construct the perpendicular bisector (see Figure 2–13). He describes the method he used: "I made the line segment then folded the paper with the line segment as the crease. I then made a point on one side and looking through the paper made a point on the other side on the point. Then I unfolded the paper and connected the point."

What seems powerful here is the seeming recognition, and use by the student, of the *invariance* of distance under reflection—fruits, one could argue, of *Investigating invariants*—as well as *Generalizing geometric ideas*—recognizing that distance is *always* preserved by reflections.

Another student tackled part 2e of the problem—the equilateral triangle—and extended the role of symmetry in the problem to point out a regular hexagon in the triangle; she writes in the lower right section: "central ∠ are =" and "create a hexagon" (see Figure 2–14).

FIGURE 2–13

i. Describe your construction method.

I made the line segment then folded the paper with the line segment on the crease. I then made a point on one side and looking through the paper made a point on the other side on the point. Then I unfolded the paper and connect the point.

FIGURE 2–14

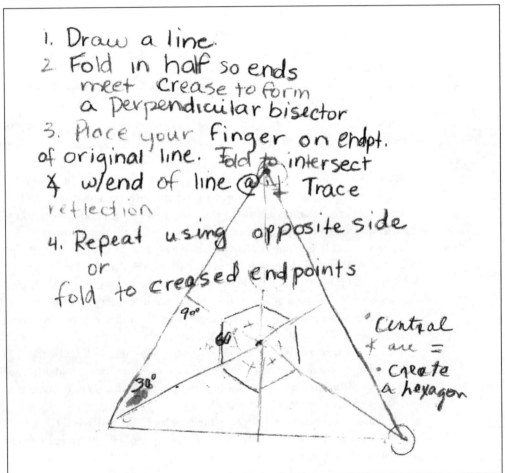

1. Draw a line.
2. Fold in half so ends meet Crease to form a Perpendicular bisector
3. Place your finger on endpt. of original line. Fold to intersect
4. w/end of line @ ⊥ Trace reflection
4. Repeat using opposite side or fold to creased endpoints

90°

60°

30°

• Central ∡ are =
• Create a hexagon

Problem 2

Another problem that can hone *Reasoning with relationships* is the following.

Infinite Reflections

Suppose you have two points in a plane, A and B. Draw a line, L, through A and take the reflection of B through L, calling it B'. If you continue this process, what can you say about the set of all the points B'?

Discussion   Engaging with this problem, at the very least, means engaging with spatial relationships—in particular, the relationship between a point and its reflected image. Other kinds of relationships can come into play as well. Indeed, the use of dynamic software on it, particularly with the trace function, can encourage both exploration and deduction, perhaps leading to a conjectured solution. Here is one way of thinking about a convincing explanation, one that makes use of congruence relationships. First, draw any line through A and locate B' (see Figure 2–15). Try the same thing with a handful of lines through A. Now eliciting a bit of *Balancing exploration and reflection*, ask yourself what you notice about the different cases—in particular, anything that is common.

Figure 2–15

Well, in each case, you might notice that B' *appears* to be the same distance from A as B is from A. Is it? Draw the segments $\overline{AB}$ and $\overline{AB'}$. It is true that reflections preserve distance, so the two right triangles in Figure 2–16 are congruent (side–angle–side), which means that $\overline{AB}$ and $\overline{AB'}$ have the same length. That piece of information implies the solution to the problem.

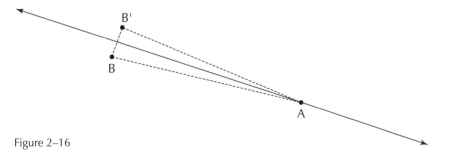

Figure 2–16

Problem 3

Congruence relationships are the focus of the following problem, but you are likely to find yourself calling forth a variety of GHOMs—in particular, *Balancing exploration and reflection*.

Versatile Vertices

Find four points in a plane that can serve as the vertices for two different but congruent quadrilaterals.

Discussion Again, dynamic software can enhance the exploration of this problem as solvers move quadrilateral vertices around to look for conjectures. *Balancing exploration and reflection* seems crucial in engaging with this problem, since it is important to reflect on features of two congruent quadrilaterals that share vertices. One might think that symmetry may play a role, and therefore would explore configurations of four points that suggest symmetry.

As the student whose paper-folded equilateral triangle demonstrated graphically, the equilateral triangle is a promising place to start. What should be added to the three existing vertices? What about the center of the triangle? (*How do you find the center?*) That promising configuration is illustrated in Figure 2–17.

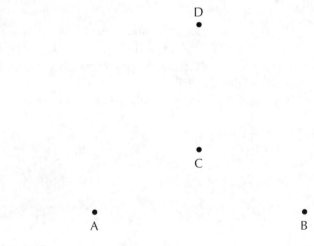

Figure 2–17

Figure 2–18 shows two congruent quadrilaterals with this set of 4 points as vertices. You should convince yourself they are indeed congruent, *and* you should seek out other sets of 4 points that also solve the problem.

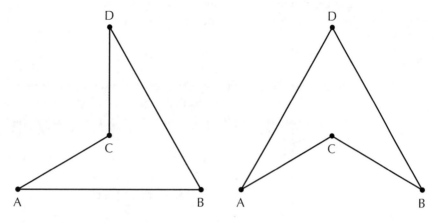

Figure 2–18

Problem 4

In middle grades, there are various geometric relationships that students need to reason about and reason with. For example, the three angles of any triangle have a particular relationship determined by the quantity of 180 degrees. Track your thinking as you reason through the following problem.

Close Triangles

Look at Figure 2–19, a triangle subdivided into 4 nonoverlapping triangles. What is the minimum number of angle measures you need to have in order to know the measures of all the angles in all 5 triangles?

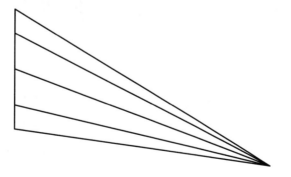

Figure 2–19

Discussion Angle exercises that middle-grades students usually see ask them to fill in the missing angles. Those exercises are valuable. However, opening up the context to ask about minimum number needed does more to problematize the issue of angles in triangles. (We have not gathered student work on this problem, so we can only speculate that this is true.)

Problem 5

Finally, it is valuable to engage in three-dimensional problems that involve geometric relationships. Problems that deal with "nets" provide contexts that link two-dimensional with three-dimensional geometric relationships, as in the following problem.

Polyhedra "Net"

If we unfold a cube and flatten it out, the resulting figure is called a "net" of the cube (see Figure 2–20). Many different nets can be formed from a given cube, depending on how you unfold it. For example, a cube also can unfold as shown in Figure 2–21.

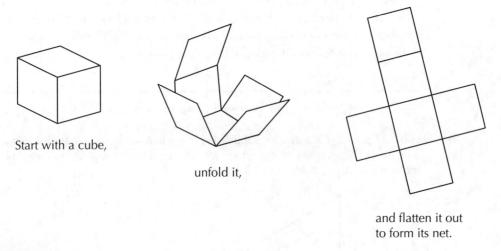

Start with a cube,

unfold it,

and flatten it out
to form its net.

Figure 2–20

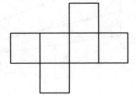

Figure 2–21

Other polyhedra, such as pyramids, have nets. A pyramid consists of a face that is a base and triangular faces that meet at a top vertex. Some sketches of pyramids are shown in Figure 2–22.

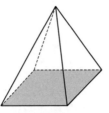

A square-based pyramid.

A hexagonal pyramid.

Figure 2–22

Construct nets for each of the following pyramids:

a. A pyramid whose base is an equilateral triangle.

b. A pyramid whose base is not an equilateral triangle.

c. A pyramid with a square base.

d. A square-based pyramid constructed so that the four triangular faces are *not* all congruent to each other.

The Sets of Nets video clip demonstrates how a group of students explored on an extended version of this problem.

Discussion   Problems involving nets require solvers to consider a range of relationships between and among figures, including boundary relationships. In addition, the transition from three-dimensional to two-dimensional representations requires some eliciting of *Investigating invariants* (e.g., consideration of what changes, what stays the same).

3

Geometric Transformations

Introduction

In the course of helping us hone geometric habits of mind (GHOM), we worked with a group of FGT Collaborating Teachers who, along with their students, worked on a variety of problems, including one that began: *Two vertices of a triangle are located at (0, 6) and (0, 12). The triangle has area 12.* Students were asked a series of questions like the following about this situation: "What are all possible positions for the third vertex?" "How do you know you have them all?" "How many of these vertices form isosceles triangles with (0, 6) and (0, 12)?"

The work sample in Figure 3–1 reveals, first of all, that this particular sixth-grade student was convinced that the third vertex could lie anywhere on two vertical lines. Many other students derived only finite sets of solution points, so this student was *Generalizing geometric ideas* at a fairly advanced level. (We also learned that many students believe that showing they "have them all" means listing them one by one, as in this student's "I don't got them all"—though she indicates the vertices can be anywhere on either vertical line. We have since changed this phrasing in problems.)

When the student reached the question about isosceles triangles, her work reveals that she apparently did a sweep of the line segment from (0, 6) to (0, 12) until it intersected the vertical lines containing all the solution points, as evidenced by the thickly drawn segments. This afforded her only an approximation of the location of the vertices in question, but it did leave her with something powerful—an existence proof that such vertices existed. We would call that an indicator of the GHOM, *Investigating invariants*, in particular, the indicator Chapter 1 described as "thinks about the effects of moving a point or figure continuously and predicts occurrences in between one point and another." This kind of thinking, which some call "reasoning by continuity" (e.g., Goldenberg, Cuoco, and Mark 1998), is a very powerful mathematical way of thinking. And, as this student demonstrates, it is accessible to middle graders in their geometric problem solving.

FIGURE 3-1

1. What are all possible positions for the third vertex? How do you know you have them all?

(4, 6) (4, 12) I don't got them all because it can be on the 4, -4 vertical line

(-4, 6) (-4, 12)

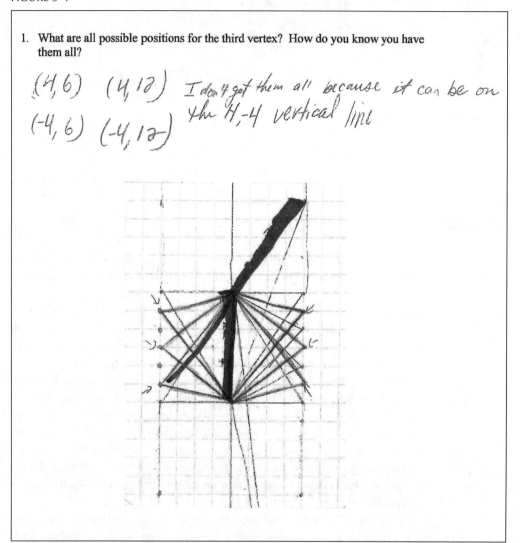

This chapter explores the power in thinking dynamically in geometry and also describes some of the hurdles middle-grades students must clear in order to engage effectively with the dynamics of geometry. Though a dynamic view of geometry has been a focus of attention for several thousands of years, since the ancients first strove to understand the movement of heavenly bodies, the recent advent and general availability of dynamic geometry software have made the ideas related to movement and transformation in geometry accessible even to middle-grades students. Take, for example, the following exploration.

Example Problem

Construct a quadrilateral ABCD and connect the midpoints of the sides. The new quadrilateral that is formed inside ABCD looks like a parallelogram. Using dynamic software one can drag points around and examine the effects of change on the figure. Doing so in random fashion (as we have done to A and B in Figure 3–2) reveals a curious fact: the interior quadrilateral continues to look like a parallelogram. Is it?

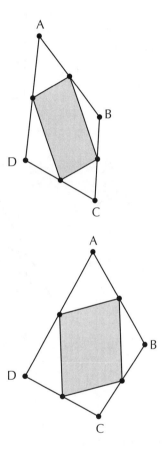

Figure 3–2

So far, we have done nothing but draw and distort figures and speculate based on perception. To see whether the speculation is correct, we can appeal to formal geometry, using knowledge of what happens when one connects the midpoints of two sides of a triangle—namely, the resulting segment is parallel to the third side. So, we construct triangles by drawing the diagonal $\overline{BD}$, getting $\triangle ABD$ and $\triangle BCD$. The segments connecting the midpoints of sides of those two triangles are each parallel with $\overline{BD}$, so they are parallel to each other (see Figure 3–3). We get a similar result for the other two sides when we connect A and C (see Figure 3–4).

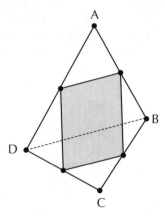

Figure 3–3

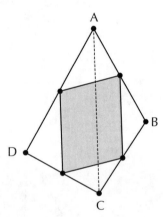

Figure 3–4

Thus, the interior quadrilateral connecting midpoints is a parallelogram. No matter how we move around the vertices of the quadrilateral, the "parallelogramness" of the interior quadrilateral will remain an invariant of the transformation. (In mathematics an *invariant* is something about a situation that stays the same, even as parts of the situation vary.)

Even middle graders can appreciate this invariance, particularly with dynamic geometry software. Although they may only appreciate it on a perceptual, speculative basis, noticing the phenomenon at all amounts to an important early engagement with the big mathematical ideas of *transformation* and *invariance*. These ideas became particularly "big" in geometry in the nineteenth century when mathematicians started developing non–Euclidean geometries.

German mathematician Felix Klein proposed to focus thinking about the different geometries by noting that each geometry is the study of invariants of a distinct group of transformations (e.g., Stillwell 2005). In Euclidean geometry, for example, length is an invariant of the group generated by translations, rotations, and reflections—the Euclidean transformations. However, in projective geometry, length is not an invariant of the corresponding group of projective transformations. (Think about a projection of a triangle to make another triangle. Usually, the side lengths are not preserved.)

The Meaning of Geometric Transformations

Loosely defined, the phrase "geometric transformation" refers to the changing of geometric figures. Quite often, as in much of this book, attention is directed to a particular figure and the results of reflecting it, rotating it, dilating it, or otherwise doing *something* dynamic to change the figure—as in the rotating of the line segment and the distortion of the quadrilateral, both described before. As a third example, in Chapter 1, we looked at what happens to the intersection of rhombus diagonals when we let the rhombus "collapse" (see Figure 3–5.)

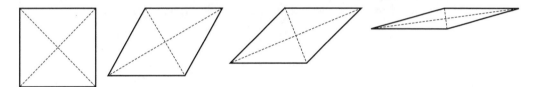

Figure 3–5

In that example, too, we saw an invariant under the dynamic change—the angle at the diagonals' intersection remained a right angle. A final example is one alluded to earlier, *dissection*, where a figure (e.g., a parallelogram) is cut into constituent pieces and then reassembled to form a different figure (e.g., a rectangle). With dissections, an invariant is the area of the figure.

In this book, we strongly advocate that students have many such opportunities to think and act dynamically in geometry. At the same time, we believe it important to emphasize special kinds of dynamic change. In the previously cited examples of changing a geometric figure, no attention is paid to points not contained in the figure or in the figure resulting from the change. In general, mathematicians attach a different and more formal meaning to geometric transformation—namely, a process that changes the entire plane or three-dimensional space (i.e., a process of mapping *every* point in a plane or three-space). As a convenient shorthand, this book uses *transform* to refer not only to these mappings but also to the other dynamic changes of figures (e.g., the moving of vertices or the "collapsing" of figures). However, we hope that teachers will work to help students understand the difference.

Learning to Think Dynamically in Geometry: Research Summary

We raise this issue of the two ways to think about change—a focus on changing individual figures versus a focus on an entire mapping of two-dimensional or three-dimensional space—because we want teachers to be alert to the conceptual difficulties experienced by some middle-grades students, tied in part to their unfamiliarity with the idea of transformation-as-mapping.

Many different types of geometric transformations, or mappings, exist; each altering some geometric properties of figures while preserving others. Euclidean transformations—translations, reflections and rotations—map points such that the original figure's position and/or orientation may be altered while its shape and size are preserved. The mapping process is different for other, non-Euclidean, transformations. Dilations, for example, map points such that a figure's size and position change while its orientation and shape do not. Figure 3–6 depicts the three Euclidean transformations, as well as dilation.

When we think of a transformation as acting on an entire plane or three-space, that process is a bit more difficult to represent with pictures. Figure 3–7 is a pictorial representation of the transformations of an entire plane of points, not just points that combine to create visible shapes or images.

FIGURE 3–6 Thick lines represent the original figures. Thin lines represent the transformations.

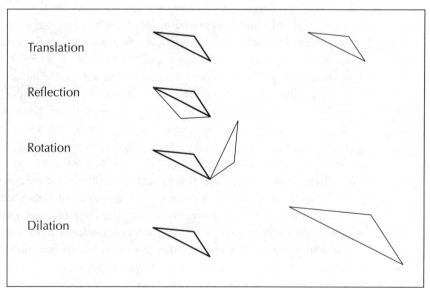

FIGURE 3–7 The parallelograms represent the plane in which the triangle lies. The solid parallelograms represent the original mapping of the plane's points and the dotted parallelograms represent the posttransformation remappings of the plane's points.

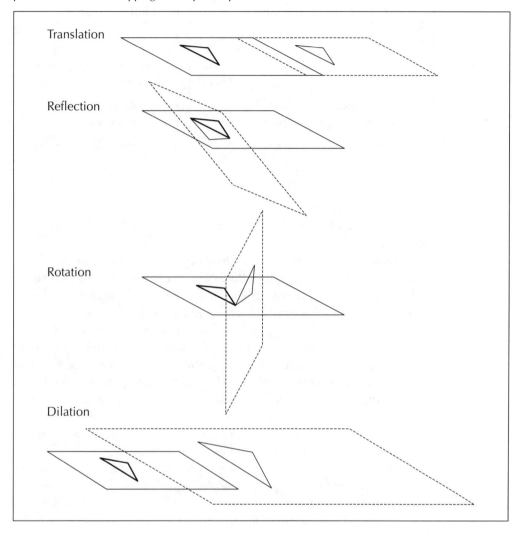

Translation

Reflection

Rotation

Dilation

What Do Geometric Transformations Mean to Middle-Grades Students?

Edwards (1991) examined middle-grades students' interactions with a computer program that afforded them an opportunity to experiment with geometric transformations. Her analysis of their behavior revealed that one-third of the students operated as if only a pictured figure, rather than the entire plane, was transformed. Interviews with these students indicated that they thought about transformations as physical motions of geometric figures rather than the mapping of an entire plane. The table in Figure 3–8 more fully delineates the differences

FIGURE 3–8

How Some Middle-Grades Students About Think Transformation	Mathematical Definition of Transformation
■ The plane is empty, invisible background.	■ The plane is a set of points.
■ Geometric figures lie on top of the plane.	■ Geometric figures are subsets of points within the plane.
■ Transformations are physical motions of geometric figure on the plane.	■ Transformations are mapping of every point in a plane.

between these students' understanding of transformations and the mathematical definition.

Students who interpret transformations as the physical motion of geometric figures are often served well by their conceptualization. For example, when centers of rotation and lines of reflection lie on the shape or figure, the position, orientation, size, and shape of the transformed figures are identical whether students map the entire plane or just the figure. It is when centers of rotation and lines of reflection are elsewhere in the plane, however, that students with this understanding have difficulty determining how to perform the transformation. Edwards found that when she asked students to use a center of rotation outside the boundaries of a figure, many translated the figure to the point of rotation before performing the rotation. As Figure 3–9 shows, a transformation performed this way, and one performed by rotating the entire plane about the point, yield figures situated in very different locations in the plane.

Regardless of whether students understand transformations to be actions carried out on figures or mapping entire planes, performing transformations can be a cognitively challenging task. A number of variables factor into the difficulty of performing a transformation. Those variables are outlined in the section that follows; it describes the cognitive processes involved in performing geometric transformations.

How Do Students Perform Geometric Transformations?

How students perform geometric transformations depends to a great extent on: (1) the amount of visual support provided, (2) the complexity of the geometric figures, and (3) students' strategy preferences.

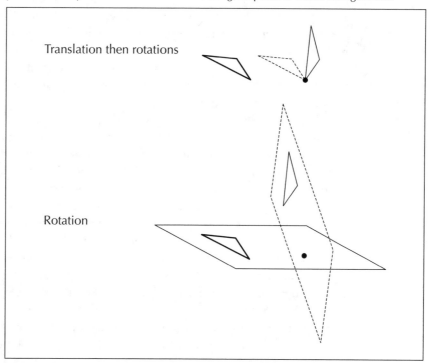

Translation then rotations

Rotation

The amount of visual support students are given when asked to perform transformations can vary. Some problems, posed at what is termed the *perceptual level*, allow solvers to manipulate geometric figures physically and therefore observe the figures throughout the transformations. A problem of this nature would be: "Create a rectangle with the square and two small triangles from the set of tangrams. Decide which transformation(s) you would perform to change the rectangle into a right triangle." In this type of problem, students could physically work with the tangram pieces as they considered possible transformations.

In contrast to these types of problems, there are those presented at what is termed the *representational level*. These types of problems display an image of the original figure but then require that the transformation be performed mentally. Solvers have minimal visual support as they work. A problem of this nature would be: "Reflect a scalene triangle over the *x*-axis and draw the resultant triangle"—a coordinate grid is pictured with a scalene triangle in the first quadrant. For this type of problem, students have a visual display of the original figure but must perform the transformation mentally.

Problems are not always posed such that they are strictly perceptual or representational in nature; that is, they have complete or minimal visual support. Some problems fall in between. They provide the original image and ask the solver to perform the transformation mentally; however, the problems do not require solvers to create the posttransformation image. Instead, several possible images are provided from which the solver can choose. A problem of this type would be similar to the one just described as representational except solvers do not have to create the transformed image.

The amount of visual support provided in a transformation activity is important because it impacts the degree to which solvers must enlist their spatial skills as they problem solve. Problems posed at the perceptual level provide substantial visual support, because they supply solvers with electronic or physical depictions of the figure throughout the transformation process. As a result, they only tax those spatial skills required for manipulating electronically or physically available objects. Problems posed at the representational level, however, provide no visual support beyond a depiction of the original figure. They rely heavily on solvers' spatial skills. Solvers must construct a mental representation of the figure; manipulate that mental representation through space; and construct the resultant figure in the appropriate orientation, location, shape, and size.

Finally, problems that fall between the perceptual and representational levels generally require solvers to construct mental representations of the original figures and to mentally manipulate those figures through space, but they do not require solvers to track figures' precise orientation, location, shape, and size, because options are provided from which to choose. Such options provide solvers with the opportunity to correct any minor miscalculations they might have made to figures' orientation, location, shape, or size while mentally operating on them.

The unique demands placed on solvers by problems at the representational level and those problems between the perceptual and representational levels are apparent in a study conducted by Kidder (1976). The study investigated middle school students' ability to (1) form mental representations of planar figures, perform mental operations on these representations, and then construct the image of the transformed figure in the proper position; (2) perform two such processes in succession; and (3) conserve the size and shape of figures during these mental transformations.

Fourth-, sixth-, and eighth-grade students were presented with a picture of a triangle, along with 10 sticks: 2 sticks equal in length to each side of the triangle and 4 distracter sticks that did not match the lengths of any of the triangle's sides (Figure 3–10). The experimenter asked students to mentally perform two consecutive transformations on the pictured triangle and to use the sticks to construct the resulting figure. Students were told that there were enough sticks to make two copies of the original triangle so that they could represent the result of the first transformation before moving into the second. Not only

FIGURE 3–10 Students were instructed to mentally perform two consecutive transformations on the pictured triangle. They were to use the sticks to depict the triangle after each transformation.

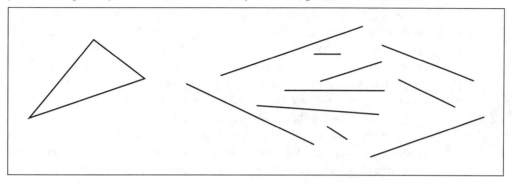

were most students unable to depict the final figure produced as a result of the composition of transformations, but they were also unsuccessful in using the sticks to depict even the first in the pair of transformations. An analysis of the figures they produced revealed that most did not even construct an image congruent to the original, much less one that was in the correct location and orientation.

When additional visual support was provided for another task, students' performance markedly improved. As part of another component to this study, students took a spatial analogy test that posed problems such that they were between the representational and perceptual levels, therefore having more visual support than the previously described task. Figure 3–11 shows an adaptation of

FIGURE 3–11

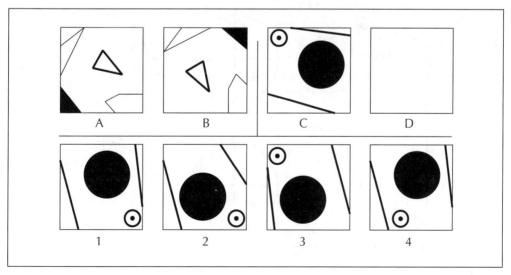

one of the questions from this test. Students determined the transformation that turned the first figure into the second and then performed that same transformation on the third figure. They then chose the image that best depicted the posttransformation figure from a set of four possibilities. Performance on this task was superior to that on the activity with sticks, suggesting processes required for this task and the sticks task are different. With an opportunity to correct orientation, location, shape, and size miscalculations after the mental transformation, students experienced a level of success markedly different from the problems posed at the representational level.

The visual support provided in a task, or the level at which a problem is posed, is not the only factor that impacts how students perform geometric transformations. The complexity of the to-be-transformed figure and a student's strategy preference are two additional important factors. Together these factors determine whether a student will employ a holistic or analytic approach to the transformation process. A *holistic approach* is defined as one in which attention is given to the figure as a whole such that mental operations are performed on intact whole figures. Students employing a holistic approach to rotate a figure by 70 degrees may mentally rotate the figure in their minds just as they would physically. With an *analytic approach*, distinct features of a figure are attended to separately, meaning that individual components of the figure are transformed at different points in time.

FIGURE 3–12 Two types of trials presented. Trials consisted of rotations of 45, 90, 135, and 180 degrees. Students were asked whether the figure on the right could be rotated to match the one on the left.

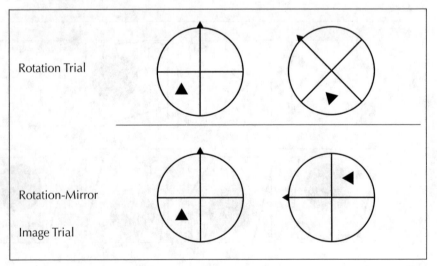

Most middle-grades students employ the holistic strategy to perform mental transformations when figures are simple. As the figures become more complex, students who are the most successful in accomplishing transformations tend to switch to an analytic approach. In this approach to problems, students convert figures into sets of features to be manipulated both spatially and logically. For example, a right triangle would be thought of in terms of its three angles and sides. Students might focus on a particular feature and ask themselves something like: "What should happen when I reflect a right angle pointing left across a vertical line?" With this strategy, the task becomes less spatial and more verbal and logical than it was with the holistic approach.

Rosser (1994) presented images like those in Figure 3–12 to fifth graders. The leftmost figure was always the same, while the other changed from trial to trial. It was either a rotated copy of the figure or a rotated mirror image of it. During the task, students pressed a button to indicate whether the figure on the right could be rotated to look like the one on the left; they were told to respond as quickly as possible. The speed at which students responded was recorded and analyzed.

The pattern of the response-time data suggests that in their attempts to determine whether the two figures were a match, half of the time students mentally rotated the figure on the right just as they would in the physical world. However, another third of the data did not fit with this particular pattern. Response time did not always increase a set amount with each increase in angular disparity. Rather, response times were longer with 45- and 135-degree clockwise rotations.

Rosser points out that, unlike with 90- and 180-degree rotations with the 45- and 135-degree rotations, three components of the figure differ in orientation—the pointers, triangles, and axes. At 90 and 180 degrees, only two components differ in orientation, the pointers and triangles. If students employed a holistic strategy to solve problems, response times should increase linearly with the angle of rotation. However, if a more analytic approach was taken in which students rotated the comparison figure one component at a time, 45- and 135-degree rotations should take longer because three components are transformed rather than two.

While a figure's complexity is important, the approach students take to do a transformation problem is not solely determined by the complexity of the figure at hand. Some students expressed a preference for the holistic or analytic approach and, therefore, gravitated toward that strategy more often than figure complexity would dictate. Boulter and Kirby (1994) videotaped a group of seventh and eighth graders as they solved a number of transformation problems, and then conducted a detailed analysis of the students' problem solving. Like Rosser (1994), they found that the complexity of the to-be-transformed figure impacted strategy choice. However, they also demonstrated that while most students use both strategies to some degree, there was substantial evidence that a portion of the students demonstrated a preference for one over the other.

Instructional Implications

The difficulty of and manner in which students perform geometric transformations depends on many factors. Teachers should examine the instructional implications related to providing varying degrees of visual support and complexity as they pose problems focused on geometric transformations. (See Table 3–1.)

TABLE 3–1   Transformations and Instructions

Concluding Points	Instructional Implications
Geometric transformations involve mapping every point in a plane, not just those points that make up figures. Many students find this a difficult concept to understand.	Conveying the idea that two-dimensional figures reside in planes and that it is the plane that is transformed, not just the figure, is especially important when centers of rotation and lines of reflection lie outside the boundaries of a figure. Teachers may want to look for ways to present the notion of a plane to students when working with these types of transformation problems.
Not all problems that ask students to perform transformations assess the same skills. Students' abilities to work with mental representations are assessed to varying degrees depending on the level at which problems are posed.	When posing transformations problems to students, teachers may want to consider how they want them to work with transformations at that particular point—physically, mentally, or mentally with the chance to check the final mental representation against a physical representation.
The complexity of a figure impacts the approach students will take in performing mental transformations. Most students use the holistic approach when translating simple figures. As figures increase in complexity, however, the students who are most successful adopt an analytic approach. They attend individually to different components of the figure and impart logic in addition to using spatial reasoning.	The different ways of approaching mental transformations are rarely presented to students; most of those who use the analytic approach discover it on their own. Students who struggle with transformations may benefit from explicit instruction related to this strategy.

Fostering GHOMs Through Problems

In addition to heeding the recommendations from the previous section, teachers can incorporate more dynamic geometry in the problems they use in the classroom. Sometimes otherwise static problems can be enriched by being given a dynamic flavor.

Problem 1

Work through the following and be aware of your thinking—especially, how you are reasoning with relationships, what role invariants have in your thinking, and how you are considering generalizations.

Sliding Down the Diagonal

Suppose point E moves along the diagonal of a square (see Figure 3–13). What is the relationship between the areas of the two shaded rectangles as E moves? Explain your thinking.

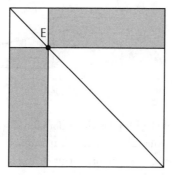

Figure 3–13

What is the relationship between the areas of the two shaded rectangles when E moves along a diagonal of a non-square rectangle? (See Figure 3–14.) Explain your thinking. What is different from the situation of the square, and what is unchanged?

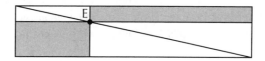

Figure 3–14

What kind of relationship exists for a non-rectangle parallelogram? (See Figure 3–15.)

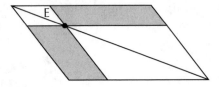

Figure 3–15

Discussion   Before moving on to the next problem, go back to the GHOM indicator lists in Chapter 1 and figure out which indicators best capture your thinking. For example, you likely found yourself *Reasoning with relationships*, relating pieces of each drawing on the basis of properties—in particular, eliciting the indicator "notices and relates configurations within a geometric figure." For example, you may have singled out the configuration in the rectangle shown in Figure 3–16 as a key to solving the problem.

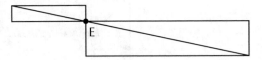

Figure 3–16

Duval (1998) provides a detailed discussion of the role that visualizing such configurations plays in the learning of geometry. It is possible, also, that you were at least wondering about how far your results *generalize*—that is, in how many kinds of polygons will the shaded regions have equal area.

Dissection problems not only are accessible to middle graders but they are also a fertile ground for developing habits of geometric thinking. In addition, we have found that when a small group of students is working on a dissection problem, something about the dynamics of the challenge makes really powerful mathematical discourse possible.

In the history of mathematics, a whole family of dissection problems have developed around the question: *What geometric figures can be dissected into congruent figures, all of which are similar to the original figure?*

Problem 2

The preceding question will be too challenging for many middle graders. However, the following problem should be accessible to most middle graders.

Similar Parts

Four copies of trapezoid ABCD, as shown in Figure 3–17, can be arranged to form a similar (and larger) trapezoid.

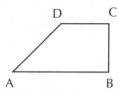 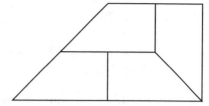

Figure 3–17

ABCD has specific measurements (shown in Figure 3–18) that enable the preceding replication to occur (and make it easy to see why the larger trapezoid is indeed similar to the smaller ones. *Why is it similar?*). Not all trapezoids have this property. (*Can you find other trapezoids that do?*)

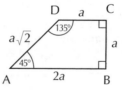

Figure 3–18

Figure 3–19 shows ΔPQR and four identical copies. Arrange the four copies of ΔPQR so as to create a triangle similar to it. (You may copy, cut out, and use the copies.) Now try the same method for ΔXYZ in Figure 3–20.

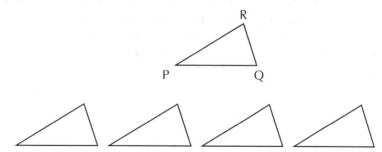

Figure 3–19

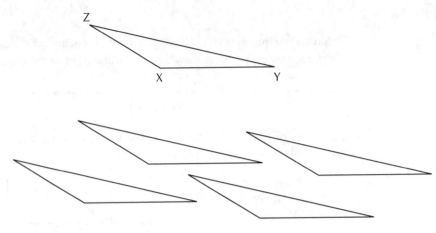

Figure 3–20

Did the same method work for both triangles? *If not, explain why not.* If so, will this method work for *any* triangle? *Provide an explanation.*

Now cut out an arbitrary triangle from a piece of patty paper. Consider this triangle to be the "final product"—that is, a large triangle that has been formed out of 4 smaller, similar triangles. Fold the paper so as to reveal the 4 smaller triangles.

Discussion The problem is structured for greater accessibility because, first, it has solvers putting pieces together, puzzlelike, then makes the dissection the *undoing* of this process. Plus, it offers a chance for the students to work backward from a final state—*Balancing exploration and reflection.*

Extension Yet another shape that has this property is shown in Figure 3–21. You can cut out the four copies of the shape and rearrange them into a larger, similar shape. The Mathematics Task Centre in Australia has developed an interesting website surrounding this particular shape (http://www.blackdouglas.com.au/ project/sphinx/sphinx.htm). There you can find numerous suggestions for extension problems and see interesting samples of student work and other resources on this so-called "Sphinx" shape.

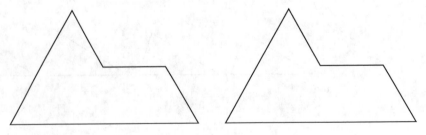

Figure 3–21

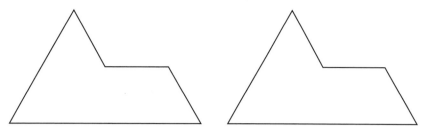

Figure 3–21 *Continued*

Rotation problems also can help foster students' GHOM development. Based on the research summary earlier in this chapter, the prompts in the problems need careful scaffolding, since many middle-grades students misunderstand when asked to rotate geometric figures around a remote center of rotation. This difficulty appears connected to the notion of a transformation as a mapping of all of two-space or three-space—a notion missing from many students' geometric understanding. This, however, does not imply that students should not have experience with such challenges.

Problem 3

We have used the Finding Centers of Rotation problem with teachers and students; it not only asks solvers to do a sequence of activities, rotating points and line segments about centers of rotation, but then also offers a tougher "undoing" challenge: Given two congruent line segments, find a center of rotation around which one segment can rotate and land squarely on the other. We have found that with appropriate supports (e.g., an animated applet demonstration of rotation) and the use of transparent paper (e.g., patty paper, wax paper, or overhead transparencies) students can engage productively with the problem.

Finding Centers of Rotation

1. Take a look at the applet at http://www.geometric-thinking.org/Rotations.htm. Explore the path a line segment takes as it rotates around a distant point.
2. Draw a point P and a line segment AB anywhere on a piece of paper. If you rotate the line segment AB around point P, what do you notice?
3. See Figure 3–22 for some pairs of congruent line segments. For each pair, find a center of rotation for rotating the line segment on the right onto the line segment on the left.

Figure 3–22

After you think you have found the center, here's a way to test to see whether your center is in the correct location:

- Place a piece of patty paper over the two segments
- Trace one of the segments and your center of rotation onto the patty paper
- Use your pencil to help anchor the patty paper at your center of rotation and rotate the patty paper to see if the traced segment will land on top of the untraced segment

Finding Centers of Rotation (clip 1) demonstrates how a group of students explored a pair of segments from part 3 of this problem.

Discussion   In our experience, middle-grades students rarely have shown themselves capable of locating the centers of rotation accurately by using strategies like looking for intersections of perpendicular bisectors. Nonetheless, productive thinking can occur. For example, Student A applied some *Balancing exploration and reflection* by using the wax paper to test candidate rotation centers, reflect, then retry (see Figure 3–23). Though the student overgeneralized on parts 1 and 2 when he got to part 4, claiming a center of rotation that is not one, on the others his method delivered accurate or close solutions.

Student B's work shows signs of both *Balancing exploration and reflection* and *Investigating invariants.* She not only experiments reflectively to locate centers of rotation, but she also seems to be aware of distance as an invariant of rotations (see Figure 3–24).

FIGURE 3–23

3. Following are some pairs of congruent line segments in the plane. For each pair, find a point of rotation for rotating the line segment on the right onto the line segment on the left and describe how you found that point.

1   The point of rotation had to be where the lines intersected so the lines can overlap. This way, you could move the lines towards each other. I knew that this would work because the quarters of a circle go straight out.

2   I found the point of rotation by guessing and checking. By using the wax paper, I found the point of rotation to be right in the center of the two lines—equal distance from each lines.

3   The point of rotation is where the lines would intersect if they were elongated. I found this by refferring back to number 1 which is basically the same problem. The quarters of a circle are straight out and of equal distance from the center point.

4   The point of rotation is where the two lines intersect just like #1 and #3.

5   I found this point of rotation by using the wax paper to make logical guesses and then checking them.

Student A

FIGURE 3–24

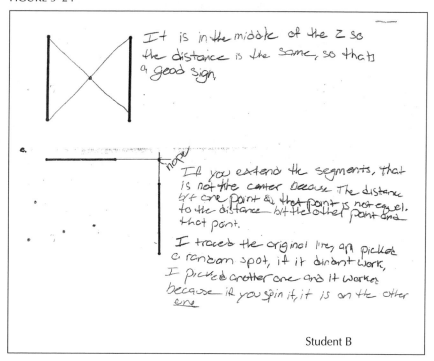

It is in the middle of the 2 so the distance is the same, so that's a good sign.

e.

more

If you extend the segments, that is not the center because The distance b/t one point & that point is not equel. to the distance b/t the other point and that point.

I traced the original lines and picked a random spot, if it didn't work, I picked another one and it worked because if you spin it, it is on the other one

Student B

Extension   For any two congruent line segments in the plane, can you find a center of rotation around which one segment can rotate to land squarely on the other? How many centers of rotation will work for two congruent segments?

Problem 4

Pivotal to the mathematical success of middle–grades students is learning how to apply the concepts of *similarity* and *proportion* to problem solving. Middle graders can engage with these concepts by *dilating* (nonmathematical term: *enlarging*) figures in two dimensions. Thus, they might be given the following problems.

Dilating Triangles

Roberto has dilated △ABC by stretching the line segment $\overline{PB}$ to B′, twice as far from P as B is; stretching $\overline{PA}$ to A′, twice as far from P as A is; and stretching $\overline{PC}$ to C′, twice as far from P as C is. Draw △A′B′C′ (see Figure 3–25). Compare △ABC and △A′B′C′. What is the same and what is different?

You will need to explain your conclusions, but before you do, look at the computer applet at http://www.geometric-thinking.org/dilations.htm. After exploring there, come to a conclusion about the two triangles and explain your conclusions.

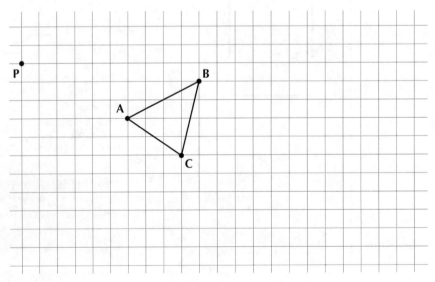

Figure 3–25

Angela dilated a triangle, using point P as her source, to make the triangle in Figure 3–26. Someone erased her original triangle. Help Angela by finding where her original triangle is located. Explain your thinking.

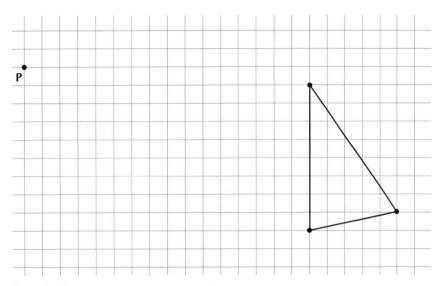

Figure 3–26

The two Dilating Triangles video clips demonstrate how a group of students explored an extended version of this problem.

Discussion   Like Problem 2, which involved dissections, this dilation problem engages solvers in a doing task, followed by an undoing task (going backward from the result of a dilation). We believe that such experiences foster flexibility in problem solvers' thinking, making it more likely that they will consider options like working backward in problems and thus enhancing their capacity for *Balancing exploration and reflection*.

Engaging with dilations problems like these, students not only can deepen their understanding of the concept of mathematical similarity but also determine that dilating a two-dimensional figure by a factor of N means that the side lengths of the new figure are N times the side lengths of the original figure and that the area of the new figure is N^2 times the area of the original figure—particular effects of dilation transformations.

Problem 5

Students can explore the generalization of the transformation effect into three dimensions with problems like the next one.

Making Similar Block Structures

Milo made a block structure with 6 blocks (see Figure 3–27). Now he wants to make a structure with the same shape (i.e., a similar shape) and with triple the dimensions of the original. How many blocks will he need? Explain how you got your answer.

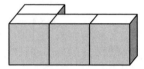

Figure 3–27

Will the same method work if Milo's original block structure is the one pictured in Figure 3–28, and he wants a structure with the same shape and with triple the dimensions? Explain why or why not the method will work, and give the total number of blocks for the new structure.

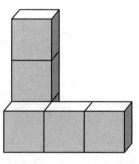

Figure 3–28

Discussion Problems like Making Similar Block Structures make it possible for students to build their capacity for *Generalizing geometric ideas* as they grow to recognize that the effect of similarity transformations on area in two dimensions generalizes to the effect of similarity transformations on volume in three dimensions. Both students and adults can struggle with envisioning "same shape and with triple the dimensions." One way of thinking about it, which we have heard expressed, exemplifies the indicator of *Balancing exploration and reflection*: "describes what the final state would look like." One person related his thinking this way: "After trying to draw pictures where I was extending each dimension, I finally imagined I already had finished enlarging it, so each one of the blocks in the picture now had eight blocks in it."

4

Geometric Measurement

The Need for Measurement Problem Solving

The Greek roots for *geometry* include the word for *earth* and the word for *measure*, making it no surprise that, in its infancy, the discipline of geometry took shape as a way to solve problems concerning the measurement of land. This chapter attends to geometric measurement in the middle grades—that is, measurement related to geometric objects such as angles, line segments, circles, spheres, polygons, polyhedra, and so on. First, however, it is important to put geometric measurement in perspective.

The Introduction to this book mentions the international comparisons in mathematics achievement—Trends in International Mathematics and Science Study (TIMSS), which focuses on grades 4, 8, and 12; and Programme for International Student Assessment (PISA), which compares the performance of 15-year-old students. A total of 24 countries participated in fourth-grade TIMSS, 45 countries participated in eighth-grade TIMSS, and 40 countries participated in PISA. Analysis of the 2003 TIMSS and PISA results (Ginsburg et al., 2005) showed that U.S. students' performance on measurement items was statistically lower than their overall score on both fourth-grade and eighth-grade TIMSS. Further, their performance on geometry items was statistically lower than their overall performance on eighth-grade TIMSS and PISA. In the opinions of the researchers, measurement and geometry were clearly U.S. students' weaknesses.

Arguably, middle graders' performance has suffered, at least in part, because of a narrow range of problem-solving experiences in geometric measurement provided by U.S. schools. Furthermore, performance seems to be particularly weak if students have come to use measurement formulas as procedures with no connections to their meaning. This chapter argues for opening up student experiences by incorporating the ideas in the previous two chapters and by eliciting and fostering the GHOMs useful in measurement problem solving.

For example, Chapter 3 advocated the benefits of thinking more dynamically in geometry problem solving—reflecting, dilating, rotating, and otherwise moving points and figures to gauge the results. Such dynamic thinking can be useful in measurement problems, particularly optimizing problems that ask for maxima or minima, for example:

→ Suppose you have a chord $\overline{AB}$ of a circle. Find the triangle inscribed in the circle with $\overline{AB}$ as a side, which has the largest area.

Before moving on, think about this problem and make note of how you are thinking about it. See whether you benefit from thinking dynamically.

A good way to start is to take advantage of the symmetry of a circle and to decide to draw the chord so that it is horizontal to the top and bottom edges of the page (see Figure 4–1). One way to think about it is: "I'll draw a triangle with $\overline{AB}$ as the base, and move the other vertex along the circle to see what happens" (see Figure 4–2).

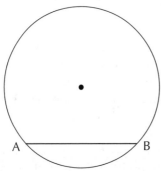

Figure 4–1

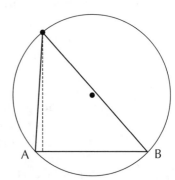

Figure 4–2

"Since Area $= \frac{1}{2}$ times altitude times length of $\overline{AB}$ for all these triangles, knowing where the altitude to $\overline{AB}$ is largest will also tell me the triangle that has the largest area." Recognition that finding the longest altitude to $\overline{AB}$ will be sufficient for finding the largest area is an example of the GHOM *Balancing exploration and reflection*—particularly marked by the indicator listed in Chapter 1: "identifies intermediate steps that can help get to the goal" (see Figure 4–3).

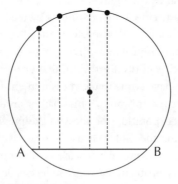

Figure 4–3

"So, the top vertex keeps rising, and the altitude keeps growing, until the vertex gets to the top of the circle, then things start getting smaller again. This gives the solution: the isosceles triangle with $\overline{AB}$ as base and with altitude passing through the center of the circle has the largest area."

→ Extension: Use this result to solve: In a circle C with radius 1, what inscribed triangle has the largest area?

Chances are, if you attempted this extension, you would be *Reasoning with relationships*—in particular, the area-based relationship between base and altitude; also symmetry relationships to reason toward the equilateral inscribed triangle. You would also be *Generalizing geometric ideas* if you used similarity relationships to reason that if the equilateral triangle has the largest area for the circle with radius 1, it also does for *any* circle. This exemplifies the fact that, at times, different GHOMs support each other to enrich geometric thinking.

Chapter 2 dealt primarily with geometric relationships, which can and should be part of students' thinking about measurement. As an example of the usefulness of this kind of opportunity for students, consider the following problem we administered to various middle-grades teachers and students: Find several different ways to calculate the area of the irregular figure in Figure 4–4.

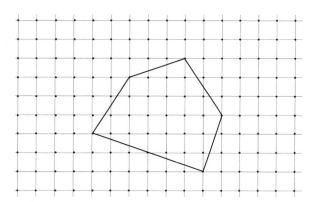

Figure 4–4

The Finding Area in Different Ways Video clip demonstrates how a group of students explored the area of another irregular figure presented in an extended version of this activity.

Many students solved it in ways similar to the student whose work is displayed in Figure 4–5. One way the student calculated area was to divide the irregular pentagon into friendlier triangles, for which it was possible to calculate the area by formula (*Reasoning with relationships* indicator: "constructs configurations within a geometric figure"). The second way, which approximated the area, amounted to dealing with the figure as a puzzle and trying to match pieces that combined into unit squares. For example, note how the two pieces labeled "9" in the bottom row seem to want to fit together to form a unit square. This

FIGURE 4–5

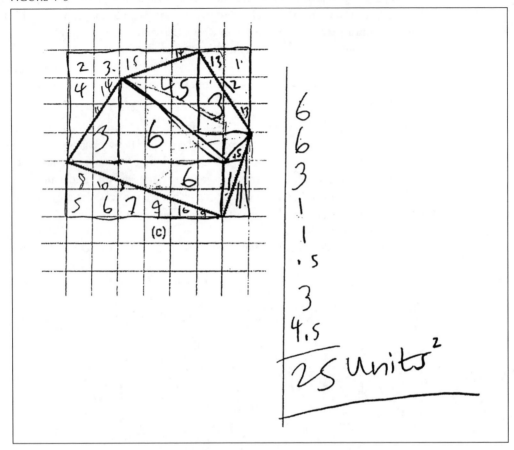

way of thinking also appears to represent the *Reasoning with relationships* indicator: "notices and relates configurations within a geometric figure."

The thinking described for the two preceding area problems (the triangle inscribed in the circle and the irregular pentagon) share an important feature—namely, both made use of the usual triangle area formula but, in each case, the use of the formula went way beyond rote procedure. It represented careful thinking about area as a space-covering measure. In our opinion, these kinds of experiences in students' learning can offset the tendency to rely on formulae only as procedures enacted in rote fashion.

Fractions and Measurement Problem Solving

Measurement models are used to help students understand fractions and computation with fractions. Generally, representing fractions in this manner is wise and useful. However, a risk exists in relying primarily on part–whole interpretation of rational numbers where the parts represented are congruent, as in ordinary pie diagrams. It allows students to count pieces, so is grounded in *additive* thinking and students tend to treat the individual parts as discrete objects. Often, this represents an overgeneralization of whole-number arithmetic. For example, if asked "Which is larger, ⅔ or ¾?" with supporting diagrams, such as the two in Figure 4–6, occasionally young middle graders will answer: "Well, I guess that they are both the same size because they both have one piece missing" (Moss 2005). They are counting the individual pieces in each diagram.

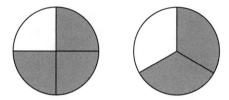

Figure 4–6

To mitigate the risk that students will overgeneralize from whole-number arithmetic and only add or subtract individual pieces, while still exploiting the potential in geometric models of fraction concepts, teachers can provide students with a variety of geometric measurement problems. Especially good are ones in which the pieces are not congruent and that can elicit the GHOM *Reasoning with relationships*; for example:

→ For each picture shown in Figure 4–7, write a fraction to show what part is shaded. For each picture, describe in pictures or words how you found that fraction, and why you believe it is the answer.

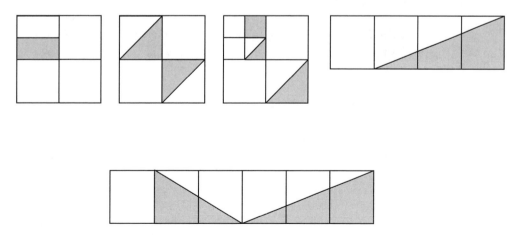

Figure 4–7

By no means do we intend to imply that this strategy will smooth all the hurdles in the course of learning rational numbers, particularly fractions. Those hurdles can be considerable. However, when students work with measurement representations of fractions, they often confront conflicts in their understanding, which observant teachers can guide them through. The following transcript is derived from the work of two sixth graders who were engaged in tangram tasks in the classroom of one of the FGT Collaborating Teachers. It begins when the students had used the 7 tangram pieces to make a rectangle, which resembled the configuration in Figure 4–8.

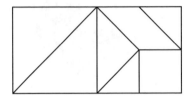

Figure 4–8

At the point where the transcript begins, the two students (S1 and S2) have made several figures, each with 3 tangram pieces and, as the teacher (T) approaches, they are starting to consider the question:

→ How does the area of each of the 3 tangram-piece figures you just made compare to the area of the rectangle you made earlier?

(*S1 and S2 construct a rectangle with all 7 tangram pieces*)
S1: First of all we know it's two parts of the whole thing.
T: *What do you mean by, "It's two parts of the whole thing"?*
S1: If you take the whole thing . . . there are seven different parts of this (rectangle they've built). Some of them may be different shapes, different sizes, but they're all equal to one part of this shape.
T: *So, would you say then that they're all one-seventh of the shape?*
S1: Yeah . . . well, no . . . kind of 'cause like this (*points to large triangle*) could be one-seventh or like if you had a greater denominator it could be greater than one-seventh 'cause it's bigger than everything else.
T: *So they're not the same size pieces, but there are seven pieces.*
S1: Yeah. And they're all one-seventh of this thing, even though some are smaller than the others.
T: *So this* (points to small triangle) *is one-seventh and this* (large triangle) *is one-seventh?*
S1: Yeah, because like this (*small triangle*) has to be at least one-seventh because you don't really go into decimals and that stuff.

T: *What do you think (calls on student S2)?*

S2: Yeah, I guess.

S1: This (*large triangle*) would also have to be one-seventh because if it was two-sevenths you'd have to remove another one of these pieces.

S2: Yeah, but what if one of the pieces was so big that it would be like half of it (*referring to the entire rectangle*)?

S1: Then you'd call that half.

. . .

T: *So is this piece (large triangle) half of your whole thing?*

S2: Two of them are.

(*S1 places large triangles on top of remaining 5 pieces that form a triangle.*)

S2: They're almost half.

S1: They're almost half of the whole thing.

T: *Do you agree with that (refers to S2)?*

S2: Yeah.

T: *Together, they're almost half of the whole thing.*

(*T moves the 2 large triangles so that they form a triangle sitting directly above the triangle formed by the remaining 5 pieces*)

S1: Oh, no, no . . . these two (*large triangles*) are equal to this part (*triangle made by 5 tangram pieces*). (*Lays 2 large triangles on top of the other 5 tangram pieces*)

S2: So those two large triangles *are* half . . . if you position it right.

S1: These two are half of the whole thing.

T: *So then, is one of them (large triangle) one-seventh of the whole thing?*

S1: Yeah, because um . . .

S2: No, one of them would be one-fourth.

Evidently, in this interaction, S1 (if not S2) is struggling with the conflict between counting pieces as equivalent units and giving each a fractional number depending on the proportion of the rectangle it covers. The former seems rooted in whole-number arithmetic; the latter is an accurate connection between an area model and fractional representation. Through her questions, the teacher appears to want to help the students push through and resolve this conflict, a very productive teaching goal in this context.

Understanding Geometric Measurement: Research Summary

In the course of their elementary and middle school years, students learn about one-dimensional measurements of length, and then are asked to apply their understanding of length to varied measurements such as the perimeter of regular and irregular shapes, side lengths, radii of circles, and diagonals of rectangles. Students then expand their notions of measurement to concepts that apply in two-dimensional space such as area or angles; and finally, they move to three-dimensional space with measurements such as volume. This research summary explores some of the common issues students face in geometric measurement.

Measuring Length

A series of three studies (Clements et al. 1997; Barrett and Clements 2003; Barrett et al. 2006) investigated how student understanding of length measurement develops. Students in the three studies were asked to do tasks such as constructing as many rectangles (or, in other cases, triangles) as they could with perimeter 24. For this task, students drew on paper and/or used a flexible straw of length 24. Table 4–1 shows a framework to focus students' understanding of the use of units in linear measurement; it emerged from observing and interviewing students during the 1997, 2003, and 2006 studies.

The last of the three studies (Barrett et al. 2006) used the levels to describe how students in three different grade bands were thinking about units of measurement:

- Students in grades 2 and 3, who were typically at levels 1 through 2b in this study, are developing their understanding of units and of how to iterate units.

- Students in grades 5 and 6, who were typically at levels 2a through 3a in this study, are beginning to generalize about units while tying their generalizations to physical representations of those units.

- Students in grades 8 through 10, who were typically at levels 2b through 3b in this study, were more likely to be able to generalize without checking physical representations.

TABLE 4–1   Development of Understanding of Length Measurement

Level 1	Uses trial and error to create shapes of a particular length. Names lengths of lines or sides without use of any particular unit.
Level 2a	Uses inconsistent units for measuring length. Counts any markers that stand out on a line to come up with a length.
Level 2b	When measuring length, consistently identifies units and/or repeats units to measure segments (e.g., using hash marks).
Level 3a	Coordinates side lengths formed by repeated units, and collections of side lengths, to obtain perimeters of objects, typically bypassing the use of hash marks.
Level 3b	Coordinates length attributes and can relate multiple cases.

One implication for these findings is that "students in grades 5 and 6 may gain confidence and expertise in measurement by being asked to reason across various cases of space figures, such as polygons, without making constant reference to physical models of each case. Students in grades 8 through 10 may benefit by having teachers probe their thinking about boundary cases and general solutions to open-ended measurement tasks" (Barrett et al. 2006, 217).

A basic example of a boundary case is a degenerate or collapsed triangle—for example, one that has sides 4, 7, and 11. This kind of concrete engagement with the relationship among triangle sides represented in the Triangle Inequality is an important opportunity for fostering the GHOM *Reasoning with relationships*. Indeed, the relationships represented in the Triangle Inequality have long been exploited to provide a bridge from geometry to probability, as in the popular question: "If you drop a spaghetti noodle and it breaks into three pieces, what is the probability that the three pieces will form a triangle?" (see, e.g., D'Andrea and Gómez 2006).

Measuring Area

Two particular ideas involved in the development of conceptual understanding about area are the mental structuring of space and the use of square units.

Mental Structuring of Space
To understand area as a measure of the space covered by an object requires mentally structuring the space of the object. Battista (1999) asked students to predict the number of square tiles they would need to cover a given rectangle. (The rectangle's sides had hash marks indicating rows and columns based on the size of the square tiles.) Students exhibited a variety of strategies, some more successful than others, when trying to determine how many square tiles were needed to cover the rectangle.

Battista characterized different developmental levels for how these students were thinking about the structuring of space, as shown in the following list. Each level builds on the one that precedes it because students can increasingly apply a mental structure to the space of the rectangle, which helps them cover the space with square units (and therefore determine its area).

1. Students do not organize the space they are structuring at all (e.g., they randomly place or draw squares within the rectangle). (See Figure 4–9.)

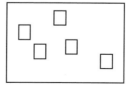

Figure 4–9

2. Students structure portions of the space, making groups of squares within the larger rectangle without being able to organize the entire space (i.e., they may group squares along the edges of the rectangle without being able to correctly locate squares in the middle of the rectangle). (See Figure 4–10.)

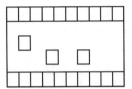

Figure 4–10

3. Students create an array of rows of squares in the rectangle but need to move the column physically to iterate it correctly. (See Figure 4–11.)

Figure 4–11

4. Students are able to abstract the rows and columns structuring the rectangle such that they can count the number of squares without drawing them or using the physical representations of them. (See Figure 4–12.)

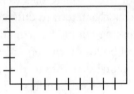

Figure 4–12

Spatial structuring issues arise as students tackle problems in three dimensions (Battista 1998) just as they do when working in two dimensions. Students must learn to mentally structure the space of three-dimensional objects by iterating identical units to measure the volumes just as they must learn to structure the space of two-dimensional objects in order to accurately measure the areas of those objects.

Connecting to the Area Formula Even if students do recognize a conceptual connection between area and measuring space, it is sometimes difficult for them to reconcile the concept with the formulas they learn for calculating area. Mitchelmore (1983) found that sixth and seventh graders could give a correct answer to areas of different rectangles, but they could not draw the unit squares in the figures (i.e., they could calculate the area but could not structure the spaces themselves).

Outhred and Mitchelmore (2000) described the progression of understanding of area according to the following levels they saw when students worked to cover space using a square tile, or without access to a square tile:

- Understanding that the area of a rectangle is based on a complete covering of that rectangle without gaps or overlaps

- Understanding that the units must be aligned in an array with the same number of units in each row

- Understanding that the number of units in each row and the number of rows can be determined based on the lengths of the sides of the rectangle

- Understanding the multiplicative structure of the array represented in the rectangle

- Understanding that the length of a line represents the number of unit lengths that will fit along it

The measurement of the area of rectangles is usually treated (even if not at the outset, eventually) as the product of two lengths (i.e., adjacent sides of the rectangle). Students who do not visualize this multiplication of two numbers as representative of a way of structuring the space taken up by the rectangle (i.e., students who have not reached the final stages in Mitchelmore's progression) see the resulting "area" as a product of two numbers rather than as a representation of an array of units (Lehrer 2003). (See Figure 4–13.)

They see the area as:
4×7

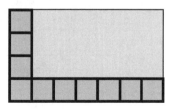

Rather than as:
4 rows × 7 units in each row

Figure 4–13

Furthermore, even if students do realize that the number of square units resulting from this multiplication of the two side lengths refers to a covering of the space of the rectangle, they do not necessarily have a mental picture of the space that accounts for those units as an array resulting from the multiplication. Instead, they may picture units of different sizes covering the space. (See Figure 4–14.)

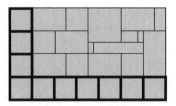

Figure 4–14

The Use of Square Units   Integral to this idea of a mental structure for the space taken up by an object is the need for appropriate and standard units of measurement that tile the plane (Lehrer 2003). Learning to use standard units (and in particular, the convention for using square units) to break up the space of objects, and therefore to measure the area of those objects, is another aspect of students' developing understanding of measurement. Students' struggles with developing a conceptual understanding of square units may stem partially from the practice of giving students square units as the standard measurement unit without giving them chances to explore what a square unit is (Lehrer 2003). Students sometimes count the number of squares without understanding that the squares represent subdivisions of a plane and without knowing why the units make good units of measurement for area.

More evidence for the need to explore and to understand the nature of appropriate units comes from observations of students who, not having been taught about square units, frequently chose units for measuring the area of a larger shape that matched the larger shape (e.g., they chose small triangles to measure a triangle and small squares to measure a square). Lehrer et al. (2003) explain that many students, especially those in elementary grades, "prefer to treat object boundaries as absolute, so that in their view, units of measure cannot in principle overlap the boundaries of the object being measured" (110),

Nitabach and Lehrer (1996) refer to this resemblance bias (i.e., the tendency to focus on the resemblance between the shape of the unit and of the object to be measured rather than on any other characteristics of the units) and point out that "developing relationships among units of measure and the attribute being measured is not trivial for students" (473). Students need opportunities to explore what a unit of area measurement is, and what makes some units better than others.

Beyond Simple Measurements of Perimeter and Area

Students who mentally structure the space covered by geometric objects, using consistent and suitable units, may still run into other struggles (e.g., confusion about connections between area and perimeter) as their notions about measurement develop. While mixing up the terms for area and perimeter does not necessarily indicate a deeper conceptual confusion, it is common for middle-grades students to believe there is a direct relationship between the area and the perimeter of shapes and this belief is more difficult to change (Furinghetti and Paola 1999; Moreira and do Rosario Contente 1997). Students need experiences that help them to see that the perimeter of a shape does not increase (or decrease) proportionally with the area. In fact, increasing the perimeter of a shape can lead to a shape with a larger area, a smaller area, or the *same* area, as exemplified in the following example.

Example   We have observed students tackling a task like: "Two vertices of a triangle are located at $(0, 2)$ and $(0, 8)$. If the area of the triangle is 12 units^2, what are all the possible positions for the third vertex?" Upon realizing that solutions extended indefinitely along the line $x = 4$, one student exclaimed: "The perimeter of triangles can get as big as you want, but the area always stays the same!"

In summary, as students learn about area, it is important to pay attention to how they think about units of measure, how they are mentally structuring space, how that structuring of space connects to their use of formulas for calculating the area of rectangles, and how they apply knowledge of area in familiar figures (e.g., rectangles) to figuring the areas of less familiar figures.

Understanding Angle

The complexity of defining and measuring angles, given students' prior experiences with measurement, combine to make the concept of angle another challenging idea in geometry. When defining angle, most middle-grades students' definitions do not incorporate the dynamic notion of rotation. Instead angles are defined by their measure or by referring to the elements involved in an angle such as line segments, rays, an intersection point, and/or the area between the rays (Keiser, Klee, and Fitch 2003). When students measure angles, once again, many do not think in terms of rotation. They search for a way to apply their previous knowledge of static measurement to situations of angle measure (Clements 2003). Some students who attempt to apply static measures to angle decide angle measure is determined by the linear distance between the two rays and/or segments of the angle. Therefore, angle size depends on length and which points along the rays and/or segments are used to perform the measurement. Other students decide angle measure is determined by the area between the rays and/or segments. Once again, angle size depends on length and where along the rays and/or segments the measurement is performed.

Keiser, Klee, and Fitch (2003) asked 77 sixth-grade students to define angle in their own words and then asked them to assess another (fictional) student's understanding of angle as it related to a particular problem. Definitions generated by students were classified according to their emphasis. Table 4–2 shows that no students made reference to the idea of rotation or turn, and that most either defined angle in terms of its measure or its static components.

After generating a definition for angle, the sixth graders were presented with a scenario in which students considered what it meant for an angle depicted on a map to be scaled up and represented in the real world. In the scenario, the majority of students decided that the angle would be much larger in the real world. Several suggested that the distance between the rays would be much greater in the real world than it was on the map.

Why Do Students Have Difficulty Defining and Measuring Angles?

Definitions students encounter often focus on one of the following ideas: (1) the union of two rays with a common endpoint (static), (2) the region contained between the two rays (static), or (3) the turning of a ray about a point from one position to another (dynamic). The first two are much more common than the third (Keiser 2004). Static representations call for linear, area, or volume measures of some sort, so students respond accordingly.

As indicated earlier, students may consider the linear distance between two rays such that the length of an angle's size depends on the length of the rays or the points along the rays used to perform the measurement. Often, students believe that the farther they travel out on the rays, the larger the angle gets. This also leads to difficulty in understanding the effects scaling has on angle. Some

TABLE 4–2   Student Definitions of Angle

Emphasis of Definition	Percentage of Students
The degrees or the measure itself: "An angle is the number of degrees in a corner."	29.5%
The line segments that meet: "An angle is where two line segments intersect to form an angle."	25.6%
The opening: "How big apart [far] the two lines are apart where the vertex is."	7.7%
The point: "An angle is where two vertices meet and make a point."	7.7%
Measure of the edge: "An angle is the measure of one side of a shape."	5.1%
Combination of two of these [the preceding]: "I think an angle is the measure in degrees between two line segments that are touching."	10.3%
Vague or wrong statements: "An angle is a shape that has straight lines and at least three angles."	14.1%

students believe that if a right angle is scaled up so that the segments of the angle are now twice as long as the original, the angle has increased as well (Keiser 2004). Finally, some students think of angle measure in terms of area between segments. All these difficulties are associated with static representations of angle and suggest that students need more exposure to dynamic representations.

Fostering GHOMs Through Geometric Measurement Problems

Students' experiences with linear measurement are often restricted to routine calculations of perimeter (in the case of circles, circumference), and these calculations usually involve little more than number addition and/or the application of formulas. Occasionally, students should be challenged to solve problems involving linear measurement.

Problem 1

Earlier in this chapter, we alluded to one such problem when describing the research in Barrett et al. (2006): *Construct as many rectangles (or triangles) as you can, with perimeter 24.* This is another linear-measurement problem.

Circular Pastures

In Round County, all pastureland is formed by circles or partial circles connected together. For example, Pasture A is made from three half circles, as seen on the map in Figure 4–15.

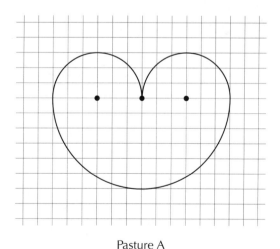

Pasture A

Figure 4–15

Pasture B is made from four half circles (see Figure 4–16).

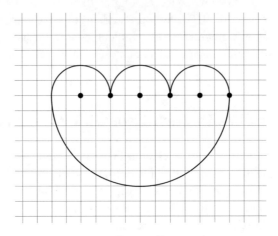

Pasture B

Figure 4–16

Pasture C is made from three half circles, but a different combination than in Pasture A (see Figure 4–17).

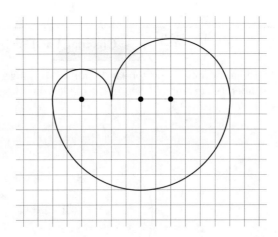

Pasture C

Figure 4–17

The owners of the three pastures need to put fencing around their pastures. Assume the fencing follows the edges of the figures that appear on the three pasture maps. How much fencing will it take for Pasture A, Pasture B, and Pasture C? How do these amounts compare with each other? Explain this relationship.

Which of these three pastures has the greatest area? The least area?

DVD

The Measuring Pastures video clip demonstrates how a group of students explored this problem.

Discussion   The equivalence of the perimeters of the three pastures is a direct result of the fact that the circumference of a circle is proportional to its diameter and of the distributive law: $\pi(d_1 + d_2 + \ldots + d_n) = \pi d_1 + \pi d_2 + \ldots \pi d_n$. So, as long as $d_1 + d_2 + \ldots + d_n =$ the diameter of the big circle, the equivalence will hold. The same is not true of area (i.e., they are not equivalent).

With this connection to proportionality and distributivity, this problem makes a connection between geometric measurement and algebra. As for GHOMs, the problem should elicit and foster *Reasoning with relationships*, especially the relationship between a circle's diameter and its circumference. Further, since the n in d_n can be as large as we want, the problem should also have students *Generalizing geometric ideas*. Finally, though there are no real transformations involved, the perimeter of these pastures is an invariant as the n in d_n gets larger and larger.

Extension   The figures representing the pastures in the problem are related to a classic figure, studied since the time of Archimedes, called the *arbelos*—the region bounded by three semicircles that are tangent in pairs with diameters that lie on the same line (i.e., the light region in Figure 4–18).

Figure 4–18

You can read more about this figure and related explorations in Boas (2006) or at http://www.arbelos.org/, which can in turn direct you to other relevant websites.

Problem 2

The beginning of the chapter advocated for engaging students in more measurement problems that invite thinking in terms of geometric relationships and thinking about geometry dynamically. This problem can serve those purposes.

Third Side Search

Many different triangles can be made with two sides of length 5 and 8. Sketch a few that are possible.

- Is it possible for the third side to have length 2? Length 7? Length 15? Why or why not?

- Which of the many possible triangles has the largest area? Explain how you arrived at your answer.

The Finding Sides of Triangles video clip demonstrates how a group of students explored an extended version of this activity.

Discussion If you and your students have access to dynamic software, this problem lends itself to that form of exploration (though explanations are still required). The first bullet requires an application of the Triangle Inequality, which in turn requires *Reasoning with relationships* (i.e., among the lengths of the sides of a triangle). The second bullet invites the same sort of reasoning used at the start of this chapter with the problem on page 72.

If you fix one of the two given sides (e.g., the one with length 8), think of the vertex joining the two given sides as a hinge, and let the other given side swing around the hinge: "What kind of motion does it make? What can this tell you about the triangle with largest area?" As in the earlier chord problem, there is *Reasoning with relationships*, especially the relationship between area of a triangle and its three base–altitude pairings. Also, if you recognized that, with the fixed side as base, it sufficed to find the greatest altitude, you were using the GHOM *Balancing exploration and reflection*, particularly the indicator listed in Chapter 1: "identifies intermediate steps that can help get to the goal."

Problem 3

The research summary earlier in this chapter implied that middle-grades students can benefit from engaging with problems that emphasize the meaning and importance of units. Here is one such problem, which also involves students in geometric transformation work.

Grid Triangles

This problem involves making triangles on a 10 × 10 dot grid. The triangles you make must have all three vertices on dots. So, the triangle in Figure 4–19 is not allowed because its top vertex doesn't lie on one of the points.

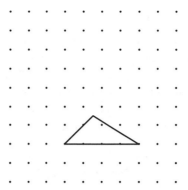

Figure 4–19

1. On a 10 × 10 dot grid, make triangles with the following areas:

   - 1 square unit
   - $\frac{3}{2}$ square units
   - 3 square units
   - 6 square units
   - 15 square units

   In each case, show how you know you have it.

2. Make as many different triangles with area 1 square unit as you can. Here, two triangles are "different" if they are not congruent.

3. Which of these area 1 triangles has the largest perimeter? Explain.

4. Draw a triangle with the largest area that can be made on the 10 × 10 dot grid. Find its area, and explain why you think it has the largest area. Are there other triangles on the 10 × 10 dot grid with the same area? Explain.

Discussion   The dot grid serves as a tool for structuring the space that area measures. It also provides a visual frame for giving meaning to the triangle area formula—A = $b \times {}^h\!/_2$. Knowledge of the Pythagorean Theorem helps, particularly for part 3, but students who don't know it or remember it can still work toward the largest perimeter of area 1 triangles through comparison and approximation. In determining how many different area 1 triangles there are on the grid, students are immersed in using knowledge of invariants under translations, rotations, and reflections—the fruits of *Investigating invariants*. Plus, of course, in judging whether two triangles are different or not, they are necessarily *Reasoning with relationships*—comparing sides and/or angles.

Problem 4

Chapter 2 mentioned the power of paper-folding problems to help students develop the capacity to reason about and with geometric relationships. Paper-folding can also enhance students' understanding of geometric measurement, particularly of area. Several helpful resources, such as Serra (1994), exist to help teachers gather appropriate problems. We have found this problem to be useful, with both teachers and students.

Investigating Area by Folding Paper

For each part of the problem, start with a square sheet of paper and make folds to construct a new shape. Then, explain how you know the shape you constructed has the specified area.

1. Construct a square with exactly ¼ the area of the original square. Explain how you know it is a square and has ¼ of the area.
2. Construct a triangle with exactly ¼ the area of the original square. Explain how you know it has ¼ of the area.
3. Construct another triangle, also with ¼ the area, that is not congruent to the first one you constructed. Explain how you know it has ¼ of the area.
4. Construct a square with exactly ½ the area of the original square. Explain how you know it is a square and has ½ of the area.
5. Construct another square, also with ½ the area, that is oriented differently from the one you constructed in 4. Explain how you know it has ½ of the area.

The Investigating Area by Folding Paper video clip demonstrates how a group of students explored part 4 of this problem.

Discussion   A wide range of GHOM influence comes into play in solving this problem. For example, in navigating parts 2 and 3, the solver needs to be adept at *Reasoning with relationships* to show why triangles are or are not congruent (e.g., in showing the two triangles in Figure 4–20 are congruent).

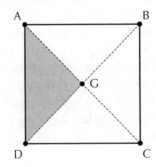
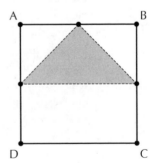

Figure 4–20

Furthermore, in generating an answer for part 3, one has to think in terms of what is *generally* true when calculating the area of triangles. For example, one might think: "If the square has side 1 and area 1, then for any triangle that fits, $\frac{1}{2} \times$ base $\times$ height $= \frac{1}{4}$. So base $\times$ height is $\frac{1}{2}$." That way of *Generalizing geometric ideas* can lead to folded constructions like those in Figure 4–21. Typically, solvers answer part 4 by folding to make the square shown in Figure 4–22.

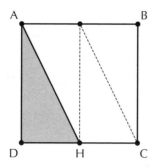

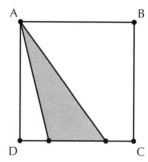

Figure 4–21

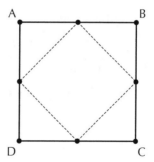

Figure 4–22

In that case, solving for part 5 can involve both *Investigating invariants* and *Balancing exploration and reflection*. The former comes into play in showing that such a square must exist without actually finding it. One can do this by imagining a point E on a diagonal of the square, say diagonal DB, close to the bottom. Connecting E to sides AD and DC with perpendicular segments forms a square (Why?). Moving E along the diagonal toward B is an action that preserves the "squareness" of the figure (Why?) but increases the area. (See Figure 4–23.)

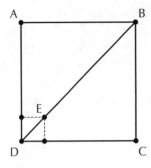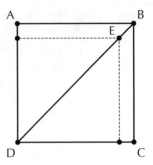

Figure 4–23

In fact, the area of the square increases from 0 to the full area of ABCD. Somewhere in between there must be a square with half the area of ABCD. This fits the indicator of *Investigating invariants:* "thinks about the effects of moving a point or figure continuously and predicts occurrences in between one point and another."

To get the exact square through paper-folding, one would need to pinpoint the size of the side of this square. Here is one way.

For simplicity, let's take the area of ABCD to be 1. Then the square in question has area ½, so must have side $\frac{1}{\sqrt{2}} = \frac{(\sqrt{2})}{2}$.

Where in the larger square might we find a length of $\frac{(\sqrt{2})}{2}$? The diagonal of ABCD is $\sqrt{2}$, so folding the diagonal in half will give a length of $\frac{(\sqrt{2})}{2}$. The following sequence of pictures shows one way to create the square out of this (see Figure 4–24).

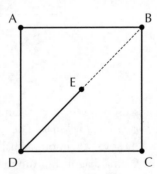

Figure 4–24

Hold D as the pivot point and fold E down to side DC, producing point F (see Figure 4–25).

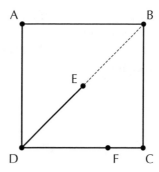

Figure 4–25

Hold D as the pivot point and fold E over to side AD, producing point G (see Figure 4–26).

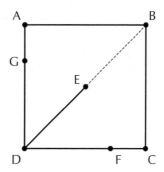

Figure 4–26

Hold F as the pivot point and fold D until it lands on diagonal DB, producing point H (see Figure 4–27).

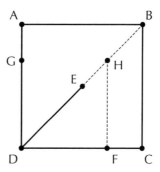

Figure 4–27

GHFD is a square with half the area of the original square. Note that the thinking about it fits the indicator of *Balancing exploration and reflection*: "describes what the final state would look like (e.g., to see whether there is any way to reason backward)."

5   *Principles for Fostering Geometric Thinking*

A major premise behind this book is that effective teaching of mathematics depends on understanding the kinds of thinking that contribute to productive learning of mathematics. We have offered the Geometric Habits of Mind (GHOM) framework as a lens on geometric thinking. In addition, we believe this framework is a valuable instructional tool, enabling translation of geometric-thinking insights into classroom action. This chapter explores the role of the GHOM framework, as well as other tools for fostering geometric thinking (FGT). It is organized under the following three principles for teaching practice:

1. Geometric thinking develops with the help of regular problem-solving opportunities.

2. Geometry in the middle grades demands special attention to teacher–student communication.

3. Middle-grades geometry is groundwork for high school geometry.

The first, in barest terms, says that we need to emphasize geometry more, especially geometric problem solving. If we are to foster middle graders' geometric thinking, then they must experience a steady diet of engaging and challenging problems. The second principle points to the special opportunities provided by geometry for teachers to attend to two essential instructional tasks: (1) helping students hone the academic language of mathematics and (2) fostering the development of geometric thinking through classroom questioning. The third principle underscores the real links that can and should be forged between students' geometry experiences in middle grades and their experiences later in formal geometry courses, particularly in conjecture and proof.

Student Geometric Thinking Develops with the Help of Regular Problem-Solving Opportunities

As noted in the Introduction, the United States lags way behind other countries in the quantity, if not the quality, of geometry instruction during the middle grades. Hence, it seems important to list the multiple reasons for sustaining a high profile for geometry and geometric thinking in middle-grades classrooms.

First of all, research in cognitive science has demonstrated that, to remember what they learn, students need to understand and actively organize what they are learning—in particular, connecting newly acquired knowledge to prior knowledge (Bransford, Brown, and Cocking 2000; Siegler 2003). In our experience, geometric problem solving provides a rich context for fostering understanding, active organization, and connections to prior knowledge. Consider a couple of examples.

Recall Chapter 3's Finding Centers of Rotation problem that asked a series of questions about rotating points around points, then raised the level of challenge by asking questions about rotating line segments—particularly asking for the center of rotation that works for rotating one given segment to another, congruent one. Recall also from Chapter 3 that rotation around remote points tends to be a foreign and difficult concept for adolescents.

The student whose work is partially reproduced in Figure 5–1 engaged in a form of spatial guess-and-check using a piece of tracing paper to try candi-

FIGURE 5–1

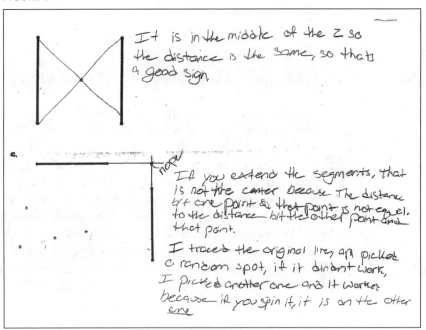

dates for center of rotation, then readjusted until one worked. Implicit in this process is an organization of what is being learned about rotational movement. Further, the student seems to have learned from rotating points about points, in the previous part of the problem, that a key feature of rotation is the invariance of the distance to the center of rotation and tried to apply this learning to the rotation of line segments. For the top pair, the student writes: "It is in the middle of the Z so the distance is the same, so that is a good sign." For the bottom pair, the student writes: "If you extend the segments, that is not the center because the distance b/t [between] one point and that point is not equal to the distance b/t the other point and that point. I traced the original line and picked a random spot. [I]f it didn't work, I picked another one and it worked because if you spin it, it is on the other one."

As a second example, consider both a problem and a student work sample you saw in Figure 4–5 in Chapter 4 (see Figure 5–2). This time examine it in light of the recommendations of cognitive science. The problem asked students to calculate the area of several irregular figures on a grid.

FIGURE 5–2

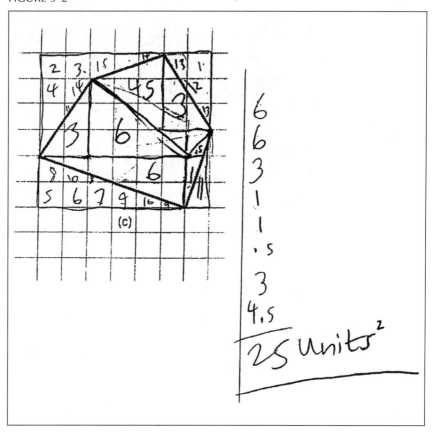

This student apparently chose to organize space in the problem by constructing familiar configurations—in this case, triangles with known base and height—that allowed him to access and use previous knowledge, namely, a formula for computing the area of a triangle.

In Chapter 1, we talked about "constructing configurations" as an indicator of the GHOM *Reasoning with relationships*. From the vantage point of cognitive science, it also can be an indicator of organizing learning. In our experience, problems in geometry and measurement in the middle grades provide numerous opportunities for such learning organization. Consider the organization a student brought to the Area 12 problem mentioned earlier:

Two vertices of a triangle are located at (0, 6) and (0, 12). The triangle has area 12. What are all possible positions for the third vertex? And how do you know you have them all? (See Figure 5–3.)

Figure 5–3

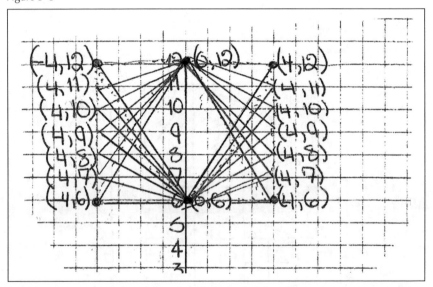

Although the student doesn't reveal whether she applied previous knowledge that reflections preserve area, it is easy to infer that she did so—drawing a triangle and then drawing its reflection through the *y*-axis.

A compelling reason to provide students a steady diet of geometry in middle grades derives from the multiple connections geometry has to other parts of mathematics. In Chapter 4, we talked briefly about the connections to probability in the context of discussing the Triangle Inequality and the traditional recreational problem: "If you drop a spaghetti noodle and it breaks into three pieces, what is the probability that the three pieces will form a triangle?" (See, for example, D'Andrea and Gómez, 2006, and the references they provide for addressing geometric probability.)

Geometry and algebra are linked in many ways. Recall that Chapter 2 began with a story about teachers working on The Staircase Problem, and how they discovered the power of having *both* algebraic and geometric solutions. As a simple example of the links to algebra, consider the following student's work, also on the Area 12 problem, in which the student is working backward with the triangle area formula to figure what the length of the triangle height must be (see Figure 5–4).

Notice that the student has apparently reversed base and height, calling H = 6—the length of the segment from (0, 6) to (0, 12)—and B = 4. This may indicate a common student misunderstanding, that "height" when applied to polygons refers only to the vertical in a pictorial representation.

Once you start to do geometry on the coordinate graph, as shown in this figure, the possible connections to algebra multiply (e.g., the connections between the concepts of similarity and slope, or the connections between vector operations and transformations like reflections and dilations).

Finally, in relation to this first recommendation, students will almost always respond to a diet of rich geometric problems with a variety of ways to approach solving them. Arguably, variety is an artifact of the visual nature of geometry, with different students attending to different features of a picture or diagram.

FIGURE 5–4

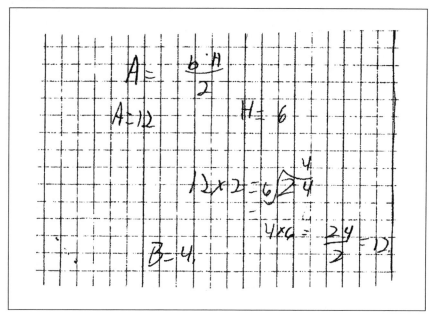

(See, for example, Duval, 1998, for a discussion of visualization in geometry.) Teachers should encourage this variety; indeed, they should occasionally encourage individual students to generate multiple ways of solving a single problem. When a prompt to generate multiple solution methods is written into problem, we often have been pleasantly surprised by the results, from students as well as teachers.

Geometry in the Middle Grades Demands Special Attention to Teacher–Student Communication

Language and Geometry

A compelling reason for giving geometry a greater presence in middle grades has to do with mathematical communication, an insight we gained as we field-tested some of the FGT ideas in an initiative sponsored by New York City's Office of English Language Learners (ELLs) to understand and close an unexplained mathematics achievement gap between ELLs and others. The initiative worked with middle school teams comprised of assistant principals, math coaches, and ESL specialists. The goal of the effort: From lesson preparation to interacting with students in the classroom to analyzing student work, each school team will be more effective in understanding evidence of difficulty with academic language as well as evidence of difficulty with mathematical concepts, and will inform the teaching and support of ELLs accordingly.

The work has been guided by a strong recommendation from research on English learners and mathematics learning to create learning environments that use *multimodal mathematical communication*—speaking, writing, diagramming, and so on—to reinforce the learning of mathematical language (e.g., Chval and Khisty 2001; Khisty and Chval 2002). We believe that geometric problem solving invites drawn, spoken, and even gestured representation of understanding, along with written verbal and written symbolic representations, and so it invites multimodal mathematical communication. For example, recall from Chapter 2 the problem pertaining to geometric dissections that first asks solvers to cut up a given parallelogram and rearrange all the pieces to make a rectangle. Then, it proceeds to tells them: "In a sequence of pictures, show where you decided to cut and how you rearranged the pieces." Next it asks: "Describe in words where you decided to cut and how you rearranged the pieces." Ultimately, "Will your method allow you to transform *any* parallelogram into a rectangle?"

Judging from experiences with the ELL teams, the transitions from pictorial to verbal explanations and from specific cases to mathematical generalization provide teachers ample opportunities to clarify and develop mathematical language for students. If you look back over the problems in the preceding chapters, you likely will agree that geometry is full of opportunities for such multimodal mathematical communication, which can benefit all students not just ELLs.

Teachers can help all students hone their knowledge of the academic language of geometry through explicit and regular modeling and clarification of language in the context of real geometric work. Once again, this can be especially helpful to ELLs, as the research of Chval and Khisty attests (Chval and Khisty 2001; Khisty and Chval 2002). The researchers' study was conducted in an urban school district in the Midwest. For more details, see The Role of Language section in Chapter 2 (pages 36–38).

Two things are noteworthy from the Chval and Khisty research. First, the teacher clarified and sharpened the geometric language within the context of mathematical work by the students. Teachers who rely totally on separate vocabulary lists to help students with language are not doing enough. Students need to learn the language in context; vocabulary lists can support this contextual clarification of language. Second, while the example pertains to ELLs, this point about contextual learning of language applies to all students.

The Power of Teacher Questioning

Teacher questioning can be a powerful tool in enabling students to understand geometry, think geometrically, and solve geometry problems, but not without the support of other skills and knowledge. First of all, the timing of questions is important, and knowing when to ask a question requires observation and listening skills, along with a good sense of what one is observing and listening *for* (see, e.g., Davis 1997).

Second, it is important to be cognizant of one's purpose in asking a question. Without an awareness of purpose, a teacher cannot clearly judge the impact of a question on student learning. Suppose, for example, that a teacher who is intent on fostering students' geometric thinking asks a student who is trying to solve a problem: "Did you consider comparing the areas of those two small triangles?" Most students will take that as a hint to compare the areas of the two small triangles and do so. Some may indeed advance their understanding by doing so, but many will not have a clue why they are singling out and comparing the two, nor will they recognize similar opportunities in the future. The teacher is unlikely to know which effect the question had, in good part because a question was posed that was really a suggestion in disguise.

In fostering geometric thinking, we have developed a simple framework to guide teachers to approach questioning purposefully. It concentrates on three kinds of questions, that we believe are germane: *orienting*, *assessing*, and *advancing*. The framework is not intended to be comprehensive (see Table 5–1). Teachers have other important purposes for asking questions; for instance, an essential purpose for some questions is *classroom management*, as when a teacher walks up

TABLE 5–1   Questioning Framework: Three Types of Questions

Question Type	Purpose	Examples
Orienting	To focus students' attention on the problem and/or on particular ways to approach the problem	What is the problem asking? Would tangrams be useful here? Do you think comparing those two sides might help? Which triangles are they asking you to compare?
Assessing	To gauge students' understanding of their statements and actions while problem solving	What do you think *congruent* means in the problem statement? Why did you fold the patty paper like that? How did you arrive at this answer? How do you know this is a rectangle?
Advancing	To help students extend their thinking toward a deeper understanding of the problem	How could you convince a skeptic that the figure you've made is a parallelogram? What if you didn't know the measure of this angle? How would you solve the problem without graph paper? What types of triangles will this work for, and why?

to a small group of students who seem disorganized and asks: "Who is the recorder in this group?" While essential in the daily flow of classroom instruction, however, such questions are somewhat removed from FGT.

Development of this framework was based on three premises:

1. It is important for teachers to be aware of purpose when asking a question and to try to align question with purpose.

2. All three types of questions play important roles in the fostering of students' geometric thinking.

3. The power of each type grows to the extent that all three types are used in balance (i.e., they support each other).

The distinctions among the question types are not always clear-cut. Indeed, the lines between them can be blurred, particularly if more than one purpose is influencing the asking of a question. So, for example, in the table we put "How do you know this is a rectangle?" under *assessing* because we imagine that the teacher is interested in finding out whether the student has an accurate conception of "rectangle."

On the other hand, we put a similar question under *advancing*: "How could you convince a skeptic that the figure you've made is a parallelogram?" It is there because we imagine that the teacher's main purpose is to induce the student to make a mathematically convincing explanation. Of course, this teacher might also want to assess whether he or she has an accurate conception of "parallelogram," but the main reason for asking it is to afford the student the opportunity to construct a convincing explanation.

The transcript that follows records a discussion held by four sixth-grade students and their teacher. Prior to it, the students had successfully completed the task of creating a non-square rectangle with seven tangram pieces. Their solution resembled the diagram in Figure 5–5. This part of their discussion pertains to the problem prompt: "Describe a way to find the area of your rectangle without using a ruler." Before going on, you should think about how you would answer this question.

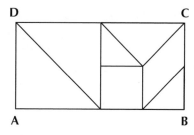

Figure 5–5

→ *Questioning exercise.* Now do an exercise we ask teachers to do after they have been exposed to the FGT Questioning Framework. Read through the transcript once to get a feel for how the students are thinking about the question and, more broadly, how they are thinking about calculating area. Then read it again; this time heed each question the teacher asks, infer the purpose or purposes behind it, and identify its type(s) based on purpose.

1. *T: So, how could you find the area. It says, "Describe a way to find the area."*
2. *S1:* You could count how many pieces are inside the object.
3. *T: So, what would you say the area of that is?*
4. *S1:* There's 5 pieces this way (*traces along the length AB of the rectangle*), and then 3 pieces this way (*traces along the width BC of the rectangle*). So 5 times 3.
5. *S2:* 15.
6. *T: Does everybody agree with that? Do you think it's 15? Tell me again why you think it's 15. Somebody repeat that and show me.*

7. *S3*: You count 1, 2, 3, 4, 5 (*counts along the length AB of the rectangle*) times 1, 2, 3 (*counts along the width BC*) . . . unless it's only 1, 2 on this side (*counts along the width AD*).

8. *S1*: It could be 10 or 15.

9. *T*: *It could be 10 or 15 . . . so . . . go ahead.*

10. *S3*: This is on the inside (*points to a shape in the interior of the rectangle*), so it wouldn't really count, so, it's only 10, right?

11. *S4*: Wait . . . there's only 2 on the side, so it should be 10.

12. *S1*: This is harder than I thought.

13. *T*: *What does area mean besides length times width? What does it tell me?*

14. *S1*: It tells you about the inside.

15. *T*: *The inside? OK. It tells me how big the inside is. So . . . do you agree with it? Is it 10? Is it 15? What is it?*

16. *S1*: I think it's 7.

17. *S2*: We can't really agree . . . we can't really know without measuring it correctly. We could give a rough estimate

18. *T*: *OK. What do you think your estimate would be?*

19. *S2*: It would be about 15 square inches.

20. *T*: *15 square inches?*

21. *S1*: Or, it could also be . . . like, since there's 7 shapes that we use, then, each shape should be 1. So 1, 2 . . . and then, if you count the sides, it makes up . . . this one doesn't really count (*points to the small tangram triangle located in the middle of the rectangle*) . . . so 1, 2, 3 . . . so it will just be 5.

22. *T*: *Are you telling me that this shape, the triangle, does not count in area?*

23. *S1*: It kind of does because the yellow point . . . every other shape has at least a full part of it (*traces the outer edge of the rectangle*), but this one (*traces small triangle in the middle of the rectangle*) is more in the middle than at the top.

24. *T*: *What did you tell me about . . . you told me two things about area. One, you told me you find it by multiplying the length times the width. But the other piece is that it's the measure of how much is inside.*

25. *S1*: Well, there's 7 inside. You could also, probably, since there's 7 shapes inside, you could multiply 7 times 2.

26. *T*: *Why would you multiply 7 times 2?*

27. *S1*: Because there's 7 shapes in here . . .

28. *S4*: . . . and 2 on the side . . .

29. *S1*: . . . and then 2 on the side . . . 2 or 3 on the side. If there's 3 on the side, then that will make 21.

30. *T*: *So, if you count it that way, there's 21? So, if I took this shape out (*removes the medium-sized tangram triangle from the rectangle*), how much of the area of 21 am I removing? Are you telling me that this is worth part of the 21?*

31. *S4*: It's worth about 3 . . . 'cause 21.

32. *S2*: (*Counting tangram pieces*) 3, 6, 9, 12, 15, 18, 21.

33. *S3:* It will be 3 plus 3 plus 3 plus 3 . . .

34. *S1:* Yep . . . it's worth 3.

35. *T: It's worth 3. So this one's worth 3* (points to the medium-sized tangram triangle)*, and the large triangle's worth 3, and the small triangle's also worth 3?*

All Students: Yes.

36. *S1:* Because, there's 7 shapes here. If you add 3 seven times, it's 21. And if you add 7 three times, it's 21.

37. *T: So you're telling me each shape is worth 3. Each shape is three twenty-firsts of the total area. Is that what you're saying?*

38. *S4:* Yes.

39. *T: OK. So you're telling me that the large triangle is taking up as much space as the small triangle?*

40. *S3:* Umm . . . yeah.

This teacher was never interviewed to get her reflections about the purposes driving her questioning, so we and you can only speculate. That said, one characterization of the interaction can be summed up as follows:

- The initial instructional purpose seems to be to help students answer the question accurately (i.e., to advance their thinking).

- Rather quickly, it appears that the teacher notices that possibly there are faulty student conceptions of area—in particular, a possible lack of coherence between the use of area formula and the idea that area "tells you about the inside" (line 14). This appears to shift the primary purpose of questioning to assessing.

- However, after asking several questions aimed at uncovering what the students' understanding of "area" is (assessment questions—lines 6, 13), the teacher starts to play a bit of devil's advocate (line 22)—an orienting move—and then throws out a question that challenges the students' organization of space by seeing how they'd respond if a piece is removed from the whole (line 30).

This kind of questioning that aims to prod students to resolve conflicts in conceptions they have has the purpose of advancing their thinking. The interaction ends with at least two or three of the students still conflicted but, arguably, closer to resolving such a conflict than they were at the start of the interaction.

Guidance in Preparing Questions

Throughout this book, we have touched on two sources of ideas for asking questions that can help foster students' geometric thinking: (1) research into learning geometry (2) the Geometric Habits of Mind (GHOM) framework. To illustrate, a few examples follow.

Chapters 2, 3, and 4 provided summaries of research, particularly findings related to student geometric misconceptions. The summaries are meant to be beneficial when forming helpful assessment and orienting questions. Consider the assessment questions the teacher in the preceding transcript asked her students, especially those about the seeming lack of alignment between their use of the formula and their conception of area as being "about the inside." A teacher cognizant of the research on students' understanding of area measurement will be prepared to ask such questions.

As another example, recall from Chapter 2 the discussion about the three types of thinking in the development of a students' concepts of geometric shape:

- *Type 1:* The student's shape concept consists of the appearance of a single prototype.

- *Type 2:* The student's shape concept consists of a single prototype and its properties.

- *Type 3:* The student's shape concept consists of many exemplars and a set of critical properties.

Recall also that an important message from research is that instruction (e.g., teacher questioning) can have a positive impact on students' progression through the types.

→ *Exercise:* For practice in devising questions, you can apply this research summary on shape concept development by watching the Dissecting Shapes (clip 2) video and by determining which questions you might ask at different points if you were watching them work on dissecting parallelograms and using the pieces to form rectangles. Be conscious of your purpose for each question.

Chapter 1 introduced the GHOMs and included with each description a set of "internal questions," which we believe are the kinds of questions productive geometric thinkers ask themselves as they solve problems.

Balancing exploration and reflection

- "What happens if I (draw a picture, add to/take apart this picture, work backward from the ending place, etc.)?"

- "What did that action tell me?"

- "How can my earlier attempts to solve the problem inform my approach now?"

- "What intermediate steps might help?"

- "What if I already had the solution . . . what would it look like?"

Reasoning with relationships

- "How are these figures alike?"

- "In how many ways are they alike?"

- "How are these figures different?"

- "What else here fits the description?"

- "What would I have to do to this object to make it like that object?"

- "What if I think about this relationship in a different dimension?"

Generalizing geometric ideas

- "Does this happen in every case?"

- "Why would this happen in every case?"

- "Have I found all the ones that fit this description?" (emphasis on *all the ones*)

- "Can I think of examples when this is not true, and, if so, should I then revise my generalization?"

- "Would this apply in other dimensions?"

Investigating invariants

- "How did that figure get from here to there?"

- "Is it possible to transform this figure so that it becomes that one?"

- "What changes? Why?"

- "What stays the same? Why?"

- "What happens to the figure if I keep applying the same transformation over and over again?"

Teachers have told us that these questions not only aid in understanding the meaning of each GHOM description but also can be turned into classroom questions by changing the direction of the question from oneself to students. Thus, "Have *I* found all the ones that fit that description?" becomes "Have *you* found all the ones that fit that description? How do *you* know?"

There is another way in which the GHOM descriptions can serve in shaping questions to ask. Recall that Chapter 1 listed some indicators of each

GHOM gathered from our work with teachers and students on numerous geometry problems; they were offered to help make the rather abstract GHOM descriptions more concrete. We hope that teachers will engage with the indicator lists in at least two ways.

First, the lists are not comprehensive, so teachers can draw from their own classroom experiences and add indicators to them. Second, teachers can use the lists as rough guides for classroom questions. For example, one of the indicators of *Balancing exploration and reflection* is "periodically returns to the big picture as a touchstone of progress." A teacher may note that a group of students is actively exploring to find a problem solution, trying this strategy then that strategy. It could help them if the teacher asked: "What you just tried . . . did that get you any closer to what the problem is asking you to do?"

→ *Side comment:* In the language of the FGT Questioning Framework in Table 5–1, this would be an *orienting* question because it seeks to focus students' attention. However, since it seeks to help students learn to balance their exploration with reflection, it also has an *advancing* quality.

Another example is that one of the indicators of *Generalizing geometric ideas* is "intuits that there are other solutions, but doesn't know how to generate them." Seeing or hearing indications that this represents a student's thinking about a problem, the teacher could ask an *advancing* question (e.g., "Can you approximate in the picture the location of another solution?").

As a final example, one of the indicators of *Reasoning with relationships* is "uses symmetry to relate geometric figures." When appropriate, a productive question is: "Can you use symmetry here?" This question often serves both to orient and to advance student thinking (i.e., it calls attention to a valuable geometric tool and helps students habituate the conscious use of the tool).

As the student work in Figure 5–6 appears to illustrate, students often take to thinking in terms of symmetry and see its value. The student was working on the Area 12 problem described earlier; she was working on the part that asked how many of the solutions are right triangles and how many are isosceles triangles. The listing of vertex coordinates suggests she was using symmetry to build her set of answers.

Middle-Grades Geometry Is Groundwork for High School Geometry

Formal proof is arguably the heart of high school geometry. Middle-grades instruction in geometry should lay the groundwork for formal proof and can do so through consistent emphasis on *convincing explanations*. Conjecturing sits

FIGURE 5–6

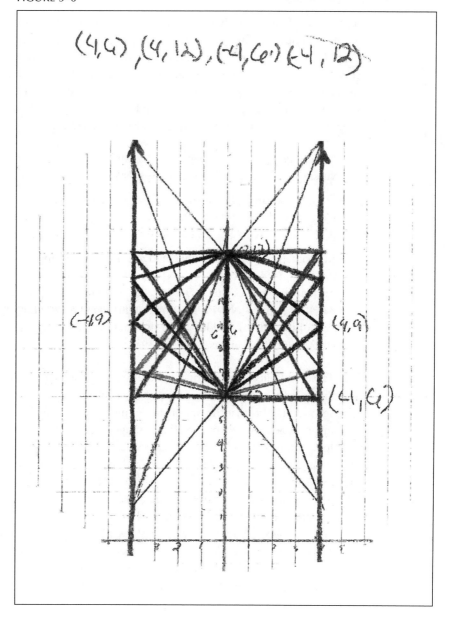

alongside proving at the heart of formal geometry. So, to prepare students to be productive "geometers" in high school, middle school educators also need to consider, along with convincing explanations, related issues such as *cognitive demand of tasks*, *development of a "geometric eye,"* and *emphasizing metacognitive development*. We discuss each of these in order.

Convincing Explanations

The work of the van Hieles and other researchers make clear that there is ample groundwork for formal deductive proof in informal deductive experiences by adolescents (Fuys, Geddes, and Tischler 1988). Student advancement therefore requires ample experience in crafting and delivering convincing explanations. Most of the problems for which we have collected work examples require students to explain procedures and convince readers of the soundness of their conclusions. The many samples we have collected suggest the following:

- Middle graders appear to have little experience in putting together convincing mathematical explanations—for geometry problems, in particular.

- Sometimes, language appears to be a barrier to writing an explanation. Consequently, as mentioned earlier in this chapter, we have altered many problems to invite pictorial as well as verbal and/or symbolic explanations.

- In geometry problems, middle graders often use perception as a warrant for their claims (e.g., the line "looks straight," or the angle is a right angle because it "has an L-shape"). Their reliance on perception likely results from a lack of familiarity with the norms and discipline of doing mathematics. Part of the role of middle-grades instruction, therefore, is to make expectations clear to students.

The first bullet suggests that middle-grades geometry instruction should provide more opportunities for students to construct convincing explanations. The second suggests that the opportunities need to be accessible to students for whom language may be a barrier. It also suggests that an important teacher role is helping students translate a pictorial explanation into one that uses the academic language of mathematics. The third bullet suggests another helpful role that teachers can play—namely, devil's advocate. It is important to ask questions that both orient students to places in their claims where they may be relying too much on perception, and advance their thinking to go beyond perception.

For example, Figures 5–7 and 5–8 show two samples of student work on parts of two different problems, the parts where the problems asked for convincing explanations. Each student did an admirable job in crafting both pictorial and verbal explanations. Both are *Reasoning with relationships* in very productive ways, as well as tapping into generalizations about geometric figures. However, the first student (see Figure 5–7) slides over the issue of whether the constructed hypotenuse is indeed a straight-line segment, saying that "You cut your rectangle into two smaller rectangles and cut one into two congruent parts diagonally. One triangle is on top. One is on the side." Then, "It contains a right angle and three vertexes, so it's a right triangle." Straightness is one of the geometric big ideas in this problem, so it is important for teachers to make explicit student thinking regarding straightness.

FIGURE 5–7

2. Without measuring, find a way to cut this rectangle into pieces you can
   rearrange to form a right triangle (final page of this problem contains a copy
   of this rectangle for you to cut).

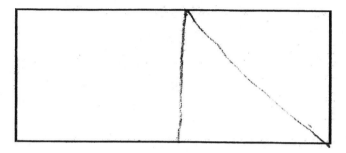

a) Describe where you decided to cut and how you rearranged the pieces.

You cut your rectangle into
two smaller rectangles, & cut
one into two congruent parts diagnlly.
One triangle is   on top one is
on the side. →

Session 6
Page 12

b) Explain how you know your final shape is a right triangle. (Consider the
   properties of the original rectangle and the cut(s) you made.)

It contains a right angle and
three vertexes, so it's a right triangle

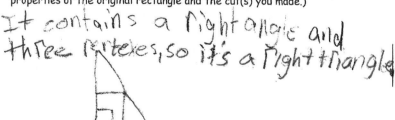

FIGURE 5–8

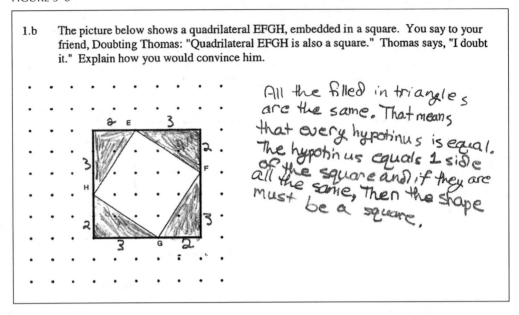

1.b   The picture below shows a quadrilateral EFGH, embedded in a square. You say to your friend, Doubting Thomas: "Quadrilateral EFGH is also a square." Thomas says, "I doubt it." Explain how you would convince him.

All the filled in triangles are the same. That means that every hypotinus is equal. The hypotinus equals 1 side of the square and if they are all the same, Then the shape must be a square.

Meanwhile, the second student (see Figure 5–8) does not provide any evidence that the angles of the quadrilateral EFGH are right angles. Given her productive use of congruence relations, she is close to having the evidence but seems to rely on perception to claim that the corners of the rhombus are right angles. Again, the concept of straightness lies underneath this problem, so it would be important for the student's teacher to help her validate her claim.

Cognitive Demand of Tasks

The FGT Questioning Framework described earlier distinguishes among orienting, assessing, and advancing types of questions. The orienting category seemed especially important to include because of a particular kind of orienting question we have observed. Many teacher questions asked in the midst of fast-paced classroom interactions effectively lead students in one direction of thought or another; quite often they direct students into ways of thinking that are strictly procedural. Sometimes this pattern of asking leading questions results from listening to students, not to understand what they are thinking but to hear an answer the teacher has predetermined to be "correct" (Davis 1997). However well intended these kinds of questions are, they very often water down tasks for students, in effect lowering the cognitive demand of the tasks.

Other actions, such as overly directive forms of task adaptation and scaffolding, can also oversimplify tasks for students. The cumulative effect of too much lowering of cognitive demand can impede student learning; or, from the perspective of this book, it can hamper the development of Geometric Habits of Mind. This conclusion about impeding learning derives from the findings of the

1995–96 QUASAR project (Silver and Stein 1996; Silver, Smith, and Nelson 1995). QUASAR, a five-year intervention in six middle schools serving poor communities, was both a school demonstration project and a complex research study of educational change and improvement. One strand focused on types of classroom mathematics tasks and on the nature of student engagement with tasks (Henningsen and Stein 1997). The researchers distinguished tasks according to *cognitive demand*. They noted that different mathematics tasks have different levels of cognitive demand and that the cognitive demand of a task can change during a lesson, depending on what teachers and students do when implementing them.

Using extensive classroom observation and analysis, along with a project-developed Cognitive Assessment Instrument, the study concluded that student-learning gains were the greatest in classrooms in which instructional tasks consistently encouraged high-level student thinking and reasoning (e.g., conjecturing, justifying, interpreting) and the least in classrooms in which instructional tasks were consistently procedural in nature.

In brief, the project led to the conclusion that, to foster *all* students' success in mathematics, teachers must support students' cognitive activity by providing a regular diet of work on meaningful tasks for which neither the complexity nor the cognitive demand is reduced (i.e., tasks that involve "doing mathematics"). The message for teachers of middle-grades geometry is clear: whether you are using tasks from your curriculum or from supplementary sources, such as this book, take care to provide a regular diet of high cognitive demand tasks for *all* students.

Development of a "Geometric Eye"

We began this book with a quote from Sir Michael Atiyah that included the sentence: "Broadly speaking I want to suggest that geometry is that part of mathematics in which visual thought is dominant whereas algebra is that part in which sequential thought is dominant." The kind of visual thought or *geometric eye* that helps in geometric problem solving can be learned through practice. Several of the listed GHOM *Reasoning with relationships* indicators mention noticing or creating configurations in geometric figures. Seeing *configurations* in figures is a form of having a geometric eye. Two attempts to figure the area of an irregular pentagon follow.

Figure 5–9 reveals a sharper geometric eye, it appears. Figure 5–10, however, reveals that the student can divide into triangle configurations, thus has the potential for a much sharper geometric eye and presumably would profit from being questioned about the choice of triangles.

The other three GHOMs also relate to having a geometric eye. For example, an indicator of *Investigating invariants* describes "thinks dynamically about a static situation." *Generalizing geometric ideas* mentions "tries generating new cases by changing features in cases already identified (e.g., applies reflections, rotations)." *Balancing exploration and reflection* lists "describes what the final state

FIGURE 5–9

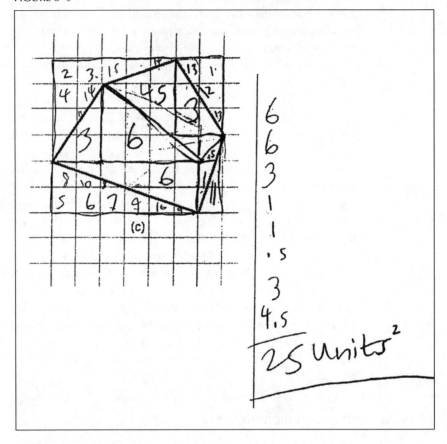

FIGURE 5–10

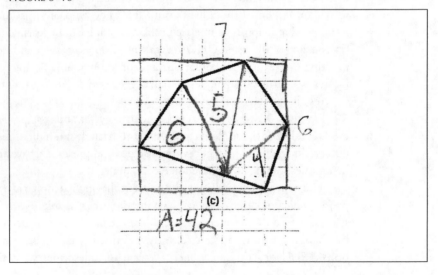

would look like (e.g., to see whether there is any way to reason backward)." Practice to sharpen the eye for configurations can take the form of the following relatively brief exercises.

How many squares can you see in Figure 5–11?

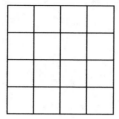

Figure 5–11

How many triangles can you see in Figure 5–12?

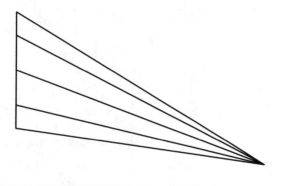

Figure 5–12

Other kinds of exercises, such as looking for symmetries in pictures or geometric diagrams, can sharpen the geometric eye. Particularly for older students, practice developing a geometric eye for three dimensions can be valuable, as in brief visualizing challenges—"Can a cube be cut by a plane so that the slice is a pentagon?"

In part, developing a geometric eye requires being able to distinguish mathematical features from nonmathematical features in problems. For a dilations problem, students used rubber band "stretchers" to dilate triangles on a grid. On one task, they were given a point P, a right triangle in bold, and three enlarged right triangles drawn in light gray. The students were asked to identify the triangle that is the result of a two-dilation of the bold triangle from P. They also were asked to "compare the original triangle with the one traced in marker. What is the same and what is different?"

The response in Figure 5–13 mixes mathematically oriented observations with those that are mathematically irrelevant (bold line versus gray line

FIGURE 5–13

The triangle traced in brown was just like a larger version of the original one. That was a similarity.

A difference is that the brown triange is bigger.
Another difference is that the brown triangle was outlined with light gray line while the original triangle was one bold line.

Both triangles are right triangles, which is a similarety.
The perimeter and area are different.
There are dots at the vertices.

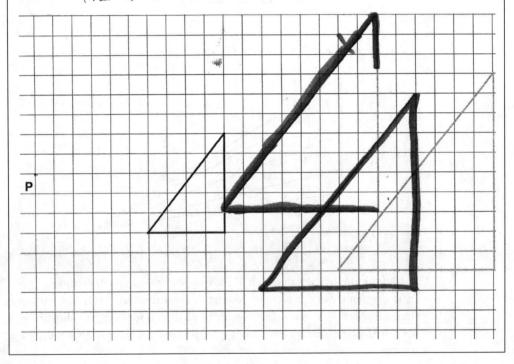

distinction). It is understandable that a middle-grades student might fail to make mathematical-nonmathematical distinctions. Nonetheless, teachers can use such data in class discussions to help students develop an eye for mathematical features.

Emphasizing Metacognitive Development

In the book *How Children Learn Mathematics in the Classroom*, the National Research Council proposed three principles for mathematics instruction, the third of which is "a metacognitive approach enables student self-monitoring" (National Research Council 2005, 236). In many ways, the book you are reading celebrates the value of the metacognitive in mathematics instruction. The GHOM framework is at the heart of the celebration in that it focuses teachers' attention on the value of thinking about thinking.

At the student level, the emphases placed on constructing convincing explanations, on distinguishing mathematical features from nonmathematical features, on taking stock during explorations, on verbal as well as pictorial representations of thinking, on responding to teacher assessment questions, and so on, all touch on different aspects of mathematical self-monitoring by students. The key to success, of course, is in the frequency with which students are encouraged to do such self-monitoring.

In an early version of a tangrams-based problem, we decided to give an extra, metacognitive task to students—namely, to finish the sentence "This makes me wonder . . ." In general, it seemed that students did not know what was expected, so we decided to drop the task. One student, however, gave us reason to want to see more unleashing of wonder in the learning of middle-grades geometry, and we close the book with that student's work (see Figure 5–14).

One could argue that this is not a profound wondering. However, by asking the simple question—"Can you make any polygon out of triangles?"—the student traveled into a space of conjecture, exploration, and generalization that is profoundly mathematical. We wish that kind of travel for all middle-grades students.

FIGURE 5–14

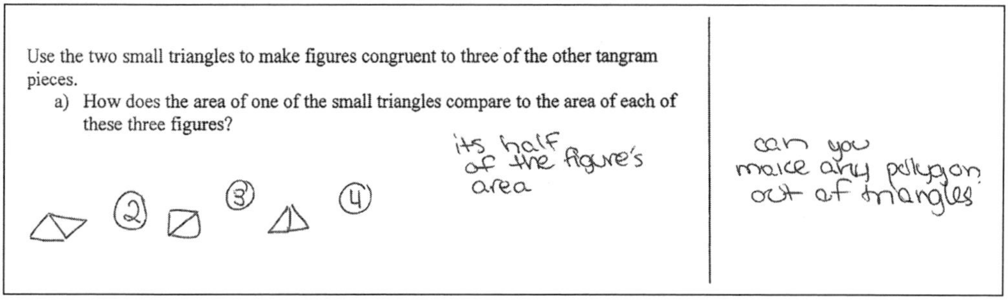

Use the two small triangles to make figures congruent to three of the other tangram pieces.
  a) How does the area of one of the small triangles compare to the area of each of these three figures?

its half of the figure's area

can you make any polygon out of triangles?

References

AAAS. 2000. *Middle Grades Mathematics Textbooks: A Benchmarks-Based Evaluation.* Washington, DC: American Association for the Advancement of Science.

Atiyah, M. 2003. "What Is Geometry?" In *The Changing Shape of Geometry: Celebrating a Century of Geometry and Geometry Teaching*, ed. C. Pritchard, 13–23. Cambridge: Cambridge University Press.

Ball, D., Hill, H., and Bass, H. 2005. "Knowing Mathematics for Teaching: Who Knows Mathematics Well Enough to Teach Third Grade, and How Can We Decide?" *American Educator* (Fall): 14–22, 43–46.

Ball, D. L., Lubienski, S. T., and Mewborn, D. S. 2001. "Research on Teaching Mathematics: The Unsolved Problem of Teachers' Mathematical Knowledge." In *Handbook of Research on Teaching.* 4th ed., ed. V. Richardson, 433–56. Washington, DC: American Educational Research Association.

Barrett, J. E., and Clements, D. H. 2003. "Quantifying Path Length: Fourth-Grade Children's Developing Abstractions for Linear Measurement." *Cognition and Instruction* 21: 475–520.

Barrett, J. E., Clements, D. H., Klanderman, D., Pennisi, S. J., and Polaki, M. V. 2006. "Students' Coordination of Geometric Reasoning and Measuring Strategies on a Fixed Perimeter Task: Developing Mathematical Understanding of Linear Measurement." *Journal for Research in Mathematics Education* 37: 187–221.

Battista, M. T. 1998. "How Many Blocks?" *Mathematics Teaching in the Middle School* 3: 404–11.

———. 1999. "The Importance of Spatial Structuring." *Teaching Children Mathematics* 6: 170–78.

Beaton, A., Mullis, I., Martin, M., Gonzalez, E., Kelly, D., and Smith, T. 1997. *Mathematics Achievement in the Middle School Years: IEA's Third International Mathematics and Science Study.* Chestnut Hill, MA: International Study Center, Lynch School of Education, Boston College.

Boas, H. P. 2006. "Reflections on the Arbelos." *The American Mathematics Monthly* 113: 236–49.

Boulter, D. R. and Kirby, J. R. 1994. "Identification of Strategies Used in Solving Transformational Geometry Problems." *Journal of Educational Research* 87: 298–303.

Bransford, J., Brown, A., and Cocking, R. 2000. *How People Learn: Brain, Mind, Experience, and School.* Washington, DC: National Academy Press.

Carpenter, T. P., Blanton, M. L., Cobb, P., Franke, M. L., Kaput, J., and McClain, K. February 2004. *Scaling Up Innovative Practices in Science and Mathematics.* Research Report. Madison, WI: National Center for Improving Student Learning and Achievement in Mathematics and Science.

Carroll, W. M. 1998. "Geometric Knowledge of Middle School Students in a Reform-Based Mathematics Curriculum." *School Science and Mathematics* 98: 188–97.

Chval, K., and Khisty, L. 2001. "Writing in Mathematics with Latino Students." Presentation at the Annual Meeting of the American Educational Research Association, April, Seattle.

Clements, D. H. 2003. "Teaching and Learning Geometry." In *A Research Companion to Principles and Standards for School Mathematics*, eds. J. Kilpatrick, W. G. Martin, and D. Schifter, 151–78. Reston, VA: National Council of Teachers of Mathematics.

Clements, D. H., and Battista, M. T. 1992. "Geometry and Spatial Reasoning." In *Handbook of Research on Mathematics Teaching and Learning: A Project of the National Council of Teachers of Mathematics*, ed. D. A. Grouws, 420–64. New York: Macmillan.

Clements, D. H., Battista, M. T., Sarama, J., and Swaminathan, S. 1996. "Development of Turn and Turn Measurement Concepts in a Computer-Based Instructional Unit." *Educational Studies in Mathematics* 30: 313–37.

Clements, D. H., Battista, M. T., Sarama, J., Swaminathan, S., and McMillen, S. 1997. "Students' Development of Length Measurement Concepts in a Logo-Based Unit on Geometric Paths." *Journal for Research in Mathematics Education* 28: 49–70.

D'Andrea, C., and Gómez, E. 2006. "The Broken Spaghetti Noodle." *The American Mathematical Monthly* 113(6): 555–57.

Davis, B. A. 1997. "Listening for Differences: An Evolving Conception of Mathematics Teaching." *Journal for Research in Mathematics Education* 28(3): 355–76.

Driscoll, M. 1999. *Fostering Algebraic Thinking: A Guide for Teachers Grades 6–10.* Portsmouth, NH: Heinemann.

Driscoll, M., Goldsmith, L., Hammerman, J., Zawojewski, J., Humez, A., and Nikula, J. 2001. *The Fostering Algebraic Thinking Toolkit.* Portsmouth, NH: Heinemann.

Duval, R. 1998. "Geometry from a Cognitive Point of View." In *Perspectives on the Teaching of Geometry for the 21st Century*, eds. C. Mammana and V. Villani, 37–52. Boston: Kluwer Academic Publishers.

Edwards, L. D. 1991. "Children's Learning in a Computer Microworld for Transformational Geometry." *Journal for Research in Mathematics Education* 22: 122–37.

Furinghetti, F., and Paola, D. 1999. "Exploring Students' Images and Definitions of Area." In *Proceedings of the 23rd PME International Conference*, ed. O. Zaslavsky, 345–52.

Fuys, D., Geddes, D., and Tischler, R. 1988. *The van Hiele Model of Thinking in Geometry Among Adolescents*. Reston, VA: National Council of Teachers of Mathematics.

Garrison, L., Amaral, O., and Ponce, G. 2006. "UnLATCHing Mathematics Instruction for English Learners." NCSM *Journal of Mathematics Education Leadership* 9(1): 14–24.

Ginsburg, A, Cooke, G., Leinwand, S., Noell, J., and Pollock, E. 2005. *Reassessing U.S. International Mathematics Performance: New Findings from the 2003 TIMSS and PISA*. Washington, DC: American Institutes for Research.

Glass, B. 2004. "Transformations and Technology: What Path to Follow?" *Mathematics Teaching in the Middle School* 9(7): 392–97.

Goldenberg, E. P., Cuoco, A. A., and Mark, J. 1998. "A Role for Geometry in General Education." In *Designing Learning Environments for Developing Understanding of Geometry and Space*, eds. R. Lehrer and D. Chazan, 3–44. Mahwah, NJ: Lawrence Erlbaum Associates.

Goldsmith, L., Mark, J., and Kantrov, I. 1998. *Choosing a Standards-Based Mathematics Curriculum*. Portsmouth, NH: Heinemann.

Golomb, S. W. 2003. "Replicating Figures in the Plane." In *The Changing Shape of Geometry: Celebrating a Century of Geometry and Geometry Teaching*, ed. C. Pritchard. Cambridge: Cambridge University Press.

Harel, G., and Sowder, L. 2005. "Advanced Mathematical Thinking at Any Age: Its Nature and Its Development." *Mathematical Thinking and Learning* 7(1): 27–50.

Henderson, D. W., and Taimina, D. 2005. *Experiencing Geometry: Euclidean and Non-Euclidean with History*. 3rd ed. Upper Saddle River, NJ: Pearson Education, Inc.

Henningsen, M., and Stein, M. K. 1997. "Mathematical Tasks and Student Cognition: Classroom-based Factors that Support and Inhibit High-Level Mathematical Thinking and Reasoning." *Journal for Research in Mathematics Education* 28(5): 524–49.

Herbst, P. G. 2006. "Teaching Geometry with Problems: Negotiating Instructional Situations and Mathematical Tasks." *Journal for Research in Mathematics Education* 37(4): 313–47.

Hershkowitz, R. 1989. "Visualization in Geometry: Two Sides of the Coin." *Focus on Learning Problems in Mathematics* 11: 61–76.

Hoyles, C., and Jones, K. 1998. "Proof in Dynamic Geometry Contexts." In *Perspectives on the Teaching of Geometry for the 21st Century*, eds. C. Mammana and V. Villani, 121–28. Boston: Kluwer Academic Publishers.

Keiser, J. M. 2004. "Struggles with Developing the Concept of Angle: Comparing Sixth-Grade Students' Discourse to the History of the Angle Concept." *Mathematical Thinking and Learning* 6(3): 285–306.

Keiser, J., Klee, A., and Fitch, K. 2003. "An Assessment of Students' Understanding of Angle." *Mathematics Teaching in the Middle School* 9: 116–19.

Kelemanik, G., Janssen, S., Miller, B., and Ransick, K. 1997. *Structured Exploration: New Perspectives on Mathematics Professional Development*. Newton, MA: Education Development Center.

Khisty, L. L., and Chval, K. 2002. "Pedagogic Discourse and Equity in Mathematics: When Teachers' Talk Matters." *Mathematics Education Research Journal* 14(3): 154–68.

Kidder, R. F. 1976. "Elementary and Middle School Children's Comprehension of Euclidean Transformations." *Journal of Research in Mathematics Education* 7: 40–52.

Lappan, G. 1999. "Geometry: The Forgotten Strand." *NCTM News Bulletin* 36(5): 3.

Lehrer, R. 2003. "Developing Understanding of Measurement." In *A Research Companion to Principles and Standards for School Mathematics*, eds. J. Kilpatrick, W. G. Martin, and D. Schifter, 179–92. Reston, VA: National Council of Teachers of Mathematics.

Lehrer, R., Jaslow, L., and Curtis, C. 2003. "Developing an Understanding of Measurement in the Elementary Grades." In *Learning and Teaching Measurement: 2003 Yearbook*, ed. D. H. Clements, 100–21. Reston, VA: National Council of Teachers of Mathematics.

Lesh, R., Lester, F. K., and Hjalmarson, M. 2003. "A Models and Modeling Perspective on Metacognitive Functioning in Everyday Situations Where Problem Solvers Develop Mathematical Constructs." In *Beyond Constructivism: Models and Modeling Perspectives on Mathematics Problem Solving, Learning, and Teaching*, eds. R. Lesh and H. M. Doerr, 383–404. Mahwah, NJ: Lawrence Earlbaum Associates.

Ma, L. 1999. *Knowing and Teaching Elementary Mathematics*. Mahwah, NJ: Lawrence Erlbaum Associates.

Martin, A. 2003. "The Sphinx Task Centre Problem." In *The Changing Shape of Geometry: Celebrating a Century of Geometry and Geometry Teaching*, ed. C. Pritchard. Cambridge: Cambridge University Press.

Mitchelmore, M. C. 1983. "Geometry and Spatial Learning: Some Lessons from a Jamaican Experience." *For the Learning of Mathematics* 3(3): 2–7.

———. 2002. "The Role of Abstraction and Generalisation in the Development of Mathematical Knowledge." In *Mathematics Education for a Knowledge-based Era: Proceedings of the Second East Asia Regional Conference on Mathematics Education and the Ninth Southeast Asian Conference on Mathematics Education*, eds. D. Edge and Y. B. Har, 157–67.

Monaghan, F. 2000. "What Difference Does It Make? Children's Views of the Differences Between Some Quadrilaterals." *Educational Studies in Mathematics* 42: 179–96.

Moreira, C. Q., and do Rosario Contente, M. 1997. "The Role of Writing to Foster Pupils' Learning About Area." In *Proceedings of the 21st Psychology of Mathematics Education International Conference*, ed. E. Pehkonen, 3: 256–63.

Moss, J. 2005. "Pipes, Tubes, and Beakers: New Approaches to Teaching the Rational-Number System." In *How Children Learn Mathematics in the Classroom*. Committee on *How People Learn: A Targeted Report for Teachers*, eds. M. S. Donovan and J. D. Bransford, 309–49. Division of Behavioral and Social Sciences and Education. Washington, DC: The National Academies Press.

Mullis, I., Martin, M., Smith, T., Garden, R., Gregory, K., Gonzalez, E., Chrostowski, S., and O'Connor, K. 2001. *TIMSS Assessment Frameworks and Specifications 2003*. Chestnut Hill, MA: TIMSS International Study Center, Boston College.

National Research Council. 2005. *How Children Learn Mathematics in the Classroom*. Committee on *How People Learn: A Targeted Report for Teachers*, eds. M. S. Donovan and J. D. Bransford. Division of Behavioral and Social Sciences and Education. Washington, DC: The National Academies Press.

NCTM. 2000. *Principles and Standards for School Mathematics*. Reston, VA: National Council of Teachers of Mathematics.

Nitabach, E., and Lehrer, R. 1996. "Developing Spatial Sense Through Area Measurement." *Teaching Children Mathematics* 2: 473–76.

Outhred, L., and Mitchelmore, M. C. 2000. "Young Children's Intuitive Understanding of Rectangular Area Measurement." *Journal for Research in Mathematics Education* 31: 144–67.

Polya, G. 1945. *How to Solve It*. Princeton, NJ: Princeton University Press.

———. 1954. *Mathematics and Plausible Reasoning: Volume 1*. Princeton, NJ: Princeton University Press.

Porter, A. 1989. "A Curriculum Out of Balance: The Case of Elementary School Mathematics." *Educational Researcher* 18: 9–15.

Powell, A. B., and Hanna, E. 2006. "Understanding Teachers' Mathematical Knowledge for Teaching: A Theoretical and Methodological Approach." In *Proceedings of the 30th Conference of the International Group for the Psychology of Mathematics Education*, July 16–21, eds. J. Novotná, H. Moraová, M. Krátká, and N. Stehlíková, 4: 369–76. Prague: Psychology of Mathematics Education.

Rosser, R. A. 1994. "Children's Solution Strategies and Mental Rotation Problems: The Differential Salience of Stimulus Components." *Child Study Journal* 24(2): 153–68.

Schwartz, J. 1999. "Can Technology Help Us Make the Mathematics Curriculum Intellectually Stimulating and Socially Responsible?" *International Journal of Computers for Mathematical Learning* 4: 99–119.

Serra, M. 1994. *Patty Paper Geometry*. Emeryville, CA: Key Curriculum Press.

Shulman, L. 1987. "Knowledge and Teaching: Foundations of the New Reform." *Harvard Educational Review* 57(1): 1–22.

Siegler, R. S. 2003. "Implications of Cognitive Science Research for Mathematics Education." In *A Research Companion to Principles and Standards for School Mathematics*, eds. J. Kilpatrick, W. B. Martin, and D. E. Schifter, 219–33. Reston, VA: National Council of Teachers of Mathematics.

Silver, E. A., Smith, M. S., and Nelson, B. S. 1995. "The QUASAR Project: Equity Concerns Meeting Mathematics Education Reform in the Middle School." In *New Directions for Equity in Mathematics Education*, eds. W. G. Secada, E. Fennema, and L. B. Adajian, 9–56. New York: Cambridge University Press.

Silver, E. A., and Stein, M. K. 1996. "The QUASAR Project: 'The Revolution of the Possible' in Mathematics Instructional Reform in Urban Middle Schools." *Urban Education* 30: 476–522.

Smith, M. S., Silver, E. A., and Stein, M. K. 2005. *Improving Instruction in Geometry and Measurement: Using Cases to Transform Mathematics Teaching and Learning*. New York: Teachers College Press.

Steen, L. 1990. *On the Shoulders of Giants: New Approaches to Numeracy*. Washington, DC: National Academy Press.

Stillwell, J. 2005. *The Four Pillars of Geometry*. New York: Springer.

Tatsuoka, K., Corker, J. E., and Tatsuoka, C. 2004. "Patterns of Diagnosed Mathematical Content and Process Skills in TIMSS-R Across a Sample of 20 Countries." *American Education Research Journal*. Winter 2004, 41(4): 901–26.

van Hiele, P. M. 1985. "The Child's Thought and Geometry." In *English Translation of Selected Writings of Dina van Hiele-Geldoff and Pierre M. van Hiele*, eds. D. Fuys, D. Geddes, and R. Tischelers, 243–52. Brooklyn, NY: Brooklyn College, School of Education.

Vygotsky, L. 1986. *Thought and Language*. Cambridge, MA: MIT Press.

Index